UNDERSTANDING
MAY SARTON

Understanding Contemporary American Literature
Matthew J. Bruccoli, Series Editor

Volumes on

Nicholson Baker • The Beats
The Black Mountain Poets • Fred Chappell
Contemporary American Drama
Contemporary American Horror Fiction
Contemporary American Literary Theory
Contemporary Chicana Literature
E. L. Doctorow • John Gardner
Lillian Hellman • Jack Kerouac
Ursula K. Le Guin • Bobbie Ann Mason
Jill McCorkle • W. S. Merwin
Arthur Miller • Toni Morrison's Fiction
Vladimir Nabokov • Gloria Naylor
Flannery O'Connor • Cynthia Ozick
Katherine Anne Porter • Reynolds Price
Annie Proulx • Thomas Pynchon
Theodore Roethke • May Sarton
Hubert Selby, Jr. • Mary Lee Settle
Jane Smiley • Robert Penn Warren • James Welch
Eudora Welty • August Wilson

UNDERSTANDING
MAY SARTON

Mark K. Fulk

University of South Carolina Press

UNIVERSITY OF SOUTH CAROLINA *BICENTENNIAL*

© 2001 University of South Carolina

Published in Columbia, South Carolina, by the
University of South Carolina Press

Manufactured in the United States of America

05 04 03 02 01   5 4 3 2 1

Library of Congress Cataloging-in-Publication Data

Fulk, Mark K., 1968–
    Understanding May Sarton / Mark K. Fulk.
      p. cm.
    Includes bibliographical references and index.
    ISBN 1-57003-422-2 (cloth : alk. paper)
    1. Sarton, May, 1912——Criticism and interpretation.
    2. Women and literature—United States—History—20th
    century. I. Title.
    PS3537.A832 Z67 2001
    811'.52—dc21   2001001661

Grateful acknowledgment is made to W. W. Norton & Company,
Inc., for permission to quote from *Collected Poems, 1930–1993*
by May Sarton. Copyright © 1993, 1988, 1984, 1980, 1974 by
May Sarton.

In memory of my grandmother Helen L. Fulk
and my aunt Myrtle E. Layton.
Both were women of Sarton's generation,
and both exhibited her qualities of endurance, strength, and joy.

CONTENTS

EDITOR'S PREFACE

The volumes of *Understanding Contemporary American Literature* have been planned as guides or companions for students as well as good nonacademic readers. The editor and publisher perceive a need for these volumes because much of the influential contemporary literature makes special demands. Uninitiated readers encounter difficulty in approaching works that depart from the traditional forms and techniques of prose and poetry. Literature relies on conventions, but the conventions keep evolving; new writers form their own conventions—which in time may become familiar. Put simply, *UCAL* provides instruction in how to read certain contemporary writers—identifying and explicating their material, themes, use of language, point of view, structures, symbolism, and responses to experience.

The word *understanding* in the titles was deliberately chosen. Many willing readers lack an adequate understanding of how contemporary literature works; that is, what the author is attempting to express and the means by which it is conveyed. Although the criticism and analysis in the series have been aimed at a level of general accessibility, these introductory volumes are meant to be applied in conjunction with the works they cover. They do not provide a substitute for the works and authors they introduce, but rather prepare the reader for more profitable literary experiences.

M. J. B.

ACKNOWLEDGMENTS

The first book of May Sarton's that I read was *Recovering* (1980), which helped me personally come to terms with grief over the death of the grandmother who raised me. Sarton's works have been gifts in this way ever since.

This volume is designed as a guide to the writings of Sarton. Divided into the broad categories of the three literary genres in which she most often wrote—poetry, novels and autobiographical writings—it considers virtually every piece Sarton published, with the exception of her writings for children. I have attempted to pay the greatest attention, however, to the works that have attracted the most sustained critical acclaim and popularity.

Thanks must go out to Simone Schroeder, a John Brown University librarian, who obtained masses of research material for me via interlibrary loan; to the research assistants Michelle Miller, Samuel Sullivan, Eva Cantu, and Scott Crain; and to the John Brown University Department of English for their continued support.

Finally, I must thank with love my father, William J. Fulk, and my wife, Angela B. Fulk. Angela has tirelessly supported me through hours of work and effort. She is my strongest critic and best support.

UNDERSTANDING
MAY SARTON

CHAPTER ONE

Understanding May Sarton

May Sarton's writing and life are characterized by candor to the point of pain and a search for an intimacy that is seldom achieved. Her vision of art centers on a search for emotional wholeness—a wholeness seated in a deep care for the spiritual, for the soul beneath the self, embracing the practices of Christian disciplines but divesting them of their traditional religious resonances. Sarton built her art upon a constant growing and maturing, emphasizing care for the soul through developing a deep sense of the sacramental power of everyday tasks, creating spaces of silence and solitude, and placing the nurture of self and others at the top of her list of priorities. In her quiet way Sarton brought the virtues of silence, simplicity, and solitude out of a religious context to make them viable for women and men who were not particularly traditional but still desired to build and foster a sense of spirituality to counteract the emotional poverty of the twentieth century. Whether in her poems, memoirs, or novels, Sarton's art nurtures the reader as the act of creating art nurtured her on her quest for wholeness, completion, and openness of self and others.

Sarton's vision—her desire for and modeling of intimacy and candor, her seeking of the highest goals for her art, and her quest for healing—comes from the pain and joys of her childhood. From her earliest age Sarton had to come to terms with separation and displacement, perhaps valuing home so much because until later in her life the location of her home was never certain. She was born on 3 May 1912 in Wondelgem, Belgium, the daughter of the historian George Sarton and the artist Eleanor Mabel Elwes Sarton. George was known for his lengthy studies of the history of science, ultimately completing a four-volume work entitled *Introduction to the History of Science* (1927). Although Sarton doted on her father, he often seemed aloof to her and was seldom at home due to difficulties at work and the shifting face of academia in the 1930s and 1940s. In a reflection on her father, written as she faces old age, Sarton writes that it has taken her a lifetime to come to terms with his relationships with her and her mother: "It took many years for me to begin to accept his lack of understanding where my mother was concerned, to accept his attitude toward me, his inability ever to discuss anything rationally where money was involved, big wounds like suddenly shouting at me, 'Why don't you get married?' when I was deeply involved with a woman with whom I could not live."[1] From her father Sarton received not only the determination she would use to write despite the odds, even into her last struggles with breast cancer, but also a distrust of men and painful fluctuations in emotions, especially in close relationships.[2]

Sarton's mother provided one of Sarton's most important relationships and an enduring, if often haunting, model of femininity. Twenty-nine years after Eleanor's death Sarton writes that her relationship with her mother was "so rare in its freedom, as though we were intimate friends rather than mother and daughter."[3] Sarton maintains that even in dying Eleanor offered her one final image of strength: "The mysterious thread will not break even when the person is at peace with herself and the world and ready to have it break in every way. But finally when my mother did die it happened so peacefully and suddenly and simply—and so it will."[4] In one of her most moving poems, "The First Autumn. For E. M. S.," Sarton sees her mother's love, like her perennial flowers, renewed in the seasons following death. This strong relationship is a key to Sarton's depiction of strong women in her works, to her own remarkable stamina, and to her haunting search for a partner as able to deal with her strengths and weaknesses as was Eleanor.

Eleanor was an artist, modeling for Sarton from an early age a woman independently pursuing an artistic calling. In the introduction to the published volume of her mother's letters, Sarton writes that her mother began her career in art as a painter of miniatures but after a nervous breakdown could no longer continue with such detailed work because her hands shook. Eleanor then launched into larger art projects, finally completing several large pieces in art deco, which were intended to be exhibited at a major art show in Belgium but were never displayed because the family had to flee the country in 1914 due to their ties with socialism.

The necessity of departing becomes a central theme in many of Sarton's novels, particularly in *The Bridge of Years* (1946), in which the family of Mélanie and Paul Duchesne flees their home in Belgium twice—once because of the German invasion in World War I and again when the Germans invade in World War II. Sarton's legacy from her mother thus provided her with an example of both a strong women and a strong relationship, yet the memory of her family is also associated with exile from Europe and the country she often fondly thought of as her home.

Thus from her family Sarton drew conclusions that perhaps many come to share in the end: namely that the wealth of love and acceptance received from families both nurtures and haunts its recipients. In a 1972 interview Sarton reflects on this equivocal heritage from her family: "I'm at the same time a tremendously emotional, aware, perhaps over-sensitive, even neurotic person *and* I am a highly disciplined person. In this combination of these two I see myself as stemming from two people who gave me very different things. My father, of course, who produced an incredible amount of work . . . did so because he was so highly disciplined and because he appreciated the value of routine. My mother, ultra-sensitive, was committed to life itself."[5] This dual legacy, when it works together well in Sarton, produces the beautiful form mixed with lyric intensity that becomes her best poetry; at its worst it produces the difficult swings of personality that plagued Sarton and disturbed some of her closest friends.[6]

While Sarton's family relocated to the United States in 1916 after traveling throughout Europe and England, Sarton did not become an American citizen until 1924. Though the flight from Belgium through England to Massachusetts made it difficult for her to find a home and feel settled, Sarton found transitional homes in her early school days and in her early career in the theater. These homes were due to the influence of formative role models Marie Closset and Eva La Gallienne. The first school Sarton attended was Shady Hill in Cambridge, Massachusetts, an open-air, all-girls school. In 1929 Sarton transferred to the High and Latin School in Cambridge for her last three years of formal schooling.

A vital episode in Sarton's education came when she was twelve years old and attending for one winter the Institut Belge de Culture Française. Here she met teacher Marie Closset, whom Sarton identifies as "one of the two or three primary influences in my life."[7] Closset, who wrote and published under the name of Jean Dominique, was one of the first people to encourage Sarton in her writing, self-assertiveness, and androgyny. Closset was often mistaken for a man in the publishing world because of her decidedly androgynous publishing name and because of her style. Sarton celebrates Closset as the heroine of her first novel, *The Single Hound* (1938), which centers on a writer's quest to find the author of a favorite collection of lyrics—an author he assumes is male but discovers is an elderly woman secluded with a group of other elderly female school teachers.

In 1926, when she was fifteen, the first significant stirring of a career came for Sarton (but not in the direction of writing): George Sarton took his daughter to see La Gallienne perform in Martinez Sierra's play *The Cradle Song*. Sarton was captivated, for this experience gave her "a vision of life."[8] That vision was not just the celebrated performance of La Gallienne or the theater itself but the sense conveyed by the theatrical company of serving "an art rather than using it for one's own ends."[9] La Gallienne, who evoked such spirit on stage, became a mentor and lifelong friend of Sarton's. Despite the consternation of her parents, Sarton convinced them to let her pursue a theater career immediately following high school. Thus in 1929 Sarton joined La Gallienne at the Civic Repertory Theater and later directed the Apprentice Theater under La Gallienne's leadership, where she remained until being forced out in 1936 due to the theater's economic hardships. La Gallienne became a mentor to Sarton in the field of her private life as well as in the theater, providing for Sarton the model of a lesbian woman devoting her life to a cause greater than a man and a marriage.

When the Civic Repertory closed in 1936 due to financial hardship, Sarton turned to writing, publishing her first two books in two years: a collection of poetry entitled *Encounter in April* (1937) and the novel *A Single Hound*. From 1937 until her death in 1995 Sarton produced fourteen books of poetry, nineteen novels, sixteen memoirs, and two books for children. Along with continuing relationships with Closset and La Gallienne, Sarton maintained several other close friendships, including those with poet Louise Bogan; academic Judy Matlack (her longtime partner and friend); Carolyn Heilbrun (her literary executor); and Susan Sherman (her friend and posthumous editor). In her almost sixty active years as a writer Sarton read and lectured at venues all over the United States. She received numerous honors, including honorary degrees from Russell Sage College, New England College, Clark University, Bates College, Colby College, University of New Hampshire, University of Maine, Bowdoin College, and Bucknell University. She also received the Golden Rose of the New England Poetry Society, the Reynolds Poetry Award, the Guggenheim Fellowship in Poetry, the Tidewater Prize, the American Academy of Arts and Sciences Fellowship, and, for her last collection, *Coming into Eighty* (1994), the Levinson Prize for Poetry.[10] Sarton, who often considered herself underappreciated by the critical and academic worlds, amassed much acclaim, a considerable number of awards, and—more important—many loyal and devoted fans.

One of the ironies of Sarton's life and art is that she, a lesbian and a solitary, never turned her back on the standard nuclear family. Indeed, as she writes in many places, she longed for just that ideal of home and family throughout her life. During the 1970s Sarton wrote a regular column for *Family Circle* and throughout her life she reviled readers and critics who wanted to read her art as advocating lesbianism or solitude over family. Sarton's art celebrates family life at the same time as it refashions it into something different, ideal, and unique. As she reflects in *After the Stroke* (1988): "I learned to be charming, to attach myself like a limpet to a rock. My love affairs have been literally 'attachments'—and when I have been happiest is when I feel at home, and what I must have always longed for is family life."[11] Stephen Robitaille describes Sarton's life as one of the most "self-documented in literary history" and one that, through living in solitude, achieved the same kind of detachment sought after in Zen Buddhist practice.[12]

Sarton's extraordinary documentation of the changes in her life is also a chronicle of the twentieth century and the writer facing these changing, contradictory times. The record Sarton leaves and the peace she at times reveals come from her commitment to this chronicling of life, making the ordinary and mundane activities of life—gardening, housekeeping, and perhaps even writing—her central focus. Sarton's steady, unwavering look at the everyday and the mundane, whether chronicled in the journals, remembered in the memoirs, or used as the substance for both poetry and novels, produces in her hands a variety of symbols of ultimate wonder and meaning. In her journal *Recovering* (1980) Sarton writes that she is "revolted by the reasons for refusing responsibilities and burdens . . . for looking upon nurturing as a somewhat contemptible task."[13] She goes on to suggest that one way around this dilemma is to embrace the ordinary, the simple, in an attempt to revalue what is truly most important: "There are some who see the sacramental side of cooking and housework."[14]

This is indeed a key to the attraction toward her art that many feel and cherish. Her nurturing and compassionate relationship to herself and others becomes central to her search for ultimate meaning in the ever-changing landscape of the twentieth century. From the detachment of her early years, leaving Europe and settling in America, to her emergence as an important American writer and one of the first women to publicly declare her lesbianism in the early 1960s, to her unremitting detail of the life of the elderly, Sarton models for many readers the life lived well. At the core of this life is her commitment to the journal form. As it evolves in Sarton's hands, the journal becomes a closer and closer chronicle of her activities and desires. Sarton's first turn toward this form comes in the rather documentary letters of her trip throughout the United States during her first poetry reading tour (1940–1941), emerges as sustained memoir and remembrance in *I Knew a Phoenix* (1954), develops into the essay collections of *Plant Dreaming Deep* (1968), and finally becomes the chronicle of her day-to-day thoughts, experiences, and reflections in her later journals.

Despite the fact that journal writing per se would most significantly evolve in Sarton's later years, this concern with chronicling the feelings, emotions, and problems she faces also factors into her definition of genre. Sarton draws an important distinction between the various modes her work encompasses. In a 1974 interview Sarton reflects on the tangible differences between her approaches to novels and poetry: "Poetry is one person's immediate feelings. It does not deal with growth and change. There are things one cannot say in poetry. Poetry does not answer to command. I have found the novel something to write when I cannot write poetry. The novel does what poetry can never do. It *must* deal with growth and change."[15] For Sarton poetry becomes momentary snatches of life lived, inspired, and written down rather quickly (although the revision process may be long). In her poetry Sarton strives to capture pure lyric, or pure light, which may be defined as the representation of a given emotion captured in a moment of time. Indeed poetry causes one to live in the moment, connecting Sarton once more with the Zen practices noted earlier. Many of her poems are occasional in nature, concerning people and events that entered her life at unexpected times and for which she had to make room as they came.

Sarton transforms the momentary into the poetic, as can be easily seen in reading her journals *Endgame* (1992) and *Encore* (1993) and the collection of poetry written alongside them, *Coming into Eighty.* In this final collection of poems Sarton relates that having to arise at three in the morning to let her kitten outdoors became the time and the inspiration leading to a series of poems, whose subjects concern the loss of friends, the washing of one's eyes, and also more global events such as the Gulf War and the death of numerous mothers and children in the Middle East. The journals chronicle the day-to-day life of this elderly woman and her reaction as she watches the Gulf War unfold, while the poetry shapes that experience into crystal-clear moments of intense emotion and wisdom.

Unlike her poetry, her journals and novels take Sarton through many mood fluctuations, which in the journals can be seen within the space of one entry or over a series of many. The journal *Recovering*, for instance, covers a period in Sarton's life when she recovers from a mastectomy and undergoes the loss of a partner due to Alzheimer's. Sarton compares journal writing with the writing of novels and poetry:

> It is true for me that the writing of a novel is that sort of tussle, and that it gives me very little pleasure while I am doing it because the effort is so great. Not so with poems that pounce out of nowhere. The writing of a poem . . . is a kind of intense trance of joy. There is no comparison.

> But I find the journal suspect because it is almost too
> easy. It is a low form of creation.[16]

Although Sarton is far too ready to dismiss the journal as an unim-
portant form of literature and a simplistic documentation of life and
history, her comparison draws out an important point: for Sarton the
novel form is about growth and demands much more effort than
either the journal or the poetic form. Sarton's novels, while center-
ing on the same concerns as her poetry and journals, remain (except
in the case of *Mrs. Stevens Hears the Mermaids Singing* [1965]) a
less valuable form in her writing than either the journals or poetry.
Her novels are problem novels that attempt to work out the difficulties of a given situation, whether it be the problems facing the
elderly, the creation of a home, or the establishment of national location and identity.

Sarton's major themes and images continue this chronicling of
life lived that comprises her art. Poetry for Sarton is the capturing of
moments, of "a kind of intense trance of joy."[17] Poetry is tied for Sarton to intense and often painful work: in a late poem entitled "The
Skilled Man" she describes the work as tireless whittling on wood;
in the poem "Pruning the Orchard" it becomes pruning to produce
fruit—a process described as sometimes "ruthless, and without a
qualm," suggesting the pain art sometimes brings.[18]

Yet this theme of facing pain exists as one of her key revelations, as a model for others and in particular as a model for women.
In a reflection on French writer Gabrielle Claudine Colette Sarton
states, "the only way through pain, and I am thinking of mental
anguish . . . is to go through it, to absorb, to probe, understand
exactly what it is and what it means. To close the door on pain is to

miss the chance for growth."[19] Sarton models in her writing and life what Heilbrun identifies as one of the most important steps toward true liberation: acknowledging one's pain fully, seeing it as a point from which to learn and grow.[20] Through Sarton's extraordinary courage in dealing with her own life and living it fully in view for her readers, she charts an identity that is candid, honest, and a model for many in the later twentieth century.

This candid and honest style often makes Sarton appear more open and intimate to readers than she actually might have been. One particular instance from her later life shows the range of the assumptions of intimacy between herself and the reader that she cultivated through her writing. In her journal *Endgame* Sarton relates the disturbing visit of a fan named Helena on 21 February 1991. This solicitous fan has sought Sarton out and, through detective work of sorts, arrived at Sarton's home in Maine with groceries unfit for Sarton's diet. Sarton finds this visit extremely threatening and intimidating, which leads her to reflect on the difference between what fans assume she is like from her art and who she really is: "Yesterday what happened was a storm of tears and a wish to commit suicide . . . because I felt there was no privacy anymore, that I simply was a *prey* to anybody who builds up this kind of obsession."[21] Sarton's honesty and openness in the journals lead to demands from readers for that same kind of intimacy in person, and the same presumption that they know more about her than perhaps they really do.

This sense of invasion reveals a person who, in her search for openness and healing, was known to be hard and difficult, perhaps demanding of others too much of what she demanded of herself. Martha M. Gordon, in her review of Margot Peters's biography of Sarton, relates an instance from the early 1980s when Sarton's temper was too apparent and Sarton revealed herself to be far from the sentimentalized figure many of her fans desired. Backstage at a poetry reading Sarton was embittered to discover that she was a second or third choice of poet to be invited and that her poetry was to be treated as the outpourings of a lesbian rather than as a more universal achievement. During the reading itself Sarton rudely waited for the removal of one fan who was occasionally coughing. Sarton readily confessed that she was really "a difficult and exasperating person" in the pursuit of her honesty and her art.[22] In writing her biography of Sarton, Peters openly faced these tensions, perhaps coming a bit too close to exploiting them for her book.[23] Sarton describes this facing of the dark elements in her self as a necessary element in the path that refines and opens us to the learning process.

Perhaps the metaphor she employs in her poem "Of Molluscs," however, suggests a darker side to her rage than Sarton herself would acknowledge; here the water that opens the mollusk in her poem would also make it prey: "As the tide rises, the closed mollusc / Opens a fraction to the ocean's food, / Bathed in its riches. Do not ask / What force would do, or if force could."[24] The sea, one of Sarton's key images, operates here as a metaphor for love. Love in Sarton's work is both wonderful and painful, both the best and worst experience of being human. Elizabeth Evans describes Sarton's art as depicting women "who can and do face and welcome their extraordinary feelings, their independent manner of living, their solitude."[25] Heilbrun explains that Sarton's solitude is not that of a misanthrope, but one of calm serenity and nurturing.[26] And yet living and spending life with someone so aware of and embroiled within those extraordinary emotions was difficult, as the host of those who knew Sarton well attest.

Solitude becomes a major theme of Sarton's art, suggesting the religious significance of a cloistered life, yet divesting it of orthodox religious meaning, and presenting it as the ideal position for a writer to reflect on her life and world. Her greatest legacy, she writes, is that of being a solitary: "If I represent anything in the public consciousness it is as a solitary. It is my solitude and what I have said about it that has made the link, and made so many women and men I do not know regard me as a friend in whom they can confide."[27] The journal form represents just this kind of solitary self contemplating individual days. The publication of journals, or even, as in Sarton's case, the writing of journals for publication, illustrates what is implicit in true solitude: the withdrawal of the self to find, contemplate, and renew that self in order to give more fully to others.

In her poem "On Sark" Sarton maps the importance and gifts of solitude. Again the sea operates as a metaphor for love, setting the inhabitants of the island Sark apart so they can be healed and nurtured. Sark comes to represent in this poem the solitary person. Sarton writes that this island exists for those who "like being surrounded by / And anchored in the ever-changing sea." The result of this island's isolated position is not only fulfillment and renewal but, beyond these, freedom of the self: "For it is just this being enclosed / In a small space within a huge space / That makes them feel safe and free / Tilling small fields under a huge sky." For the solitary, solitude is not "being alone / Is not loneliness but fertile good." In the third stanza Sarton brings herself into this otherwise descriptive nature poem. She writes that here, on Sark and in solitude, she is "myself at home." Yet this feeling of safety, security, and freedom is not valued for its own sake but for what it results in, which is the ability to return again to love and to loving others. In her final stanza Sarton reflects that she too is ready to return to love: "I am ready to begin the long journey / Toward love, the mainland, perhaps not alone."[28] Solitude in Sarton's writing ultimately exists for the sake of giving back to others a fuller, more complete self through love.

As a result of returning from a time of solitude, Sarton considers what it means to love and what it means to seek family, whether in marriage or through intense friendships. The poetry in *Halfway to Silence* (1980) recognizes that, sadly, in our less-than-perfect state, love often contains elements of brutality and violence. Yet Sarton's honest recognition of these elements does not lead her toward cynicism, but instead toward an honest optimism about love and bonding. In her poem "Love," love becomes the fragile web of a spider, often torn and often repaired. "Spiders," Sarton comments, "are patient weavers. / They never give up."[29] It is important to note that Sarton has here set herself up for a sentimental ending that could in effect mar the poem and elide the very dangers and pitfalls of love she has set out to explore. A master of lyric, though, Sarton leaves intact both an optimistic if perhaps sentimental reading of love and the real issue—that we need to be loved. Her final description concerns why the spider remains a patient weaver in the same way that we remain patient in our seeking for and offering of love: "And who knows / What keeps them at it? / Hunger, no doubt, / And hope."[30]

In her journals Sarton recognizes the more dangerous aspects of love. She begins one of her later journals, *Recovering,* in order to celebrate her long-term relationship with Matlack, which is coming to an end. Sarton recognizes in this journal that many readers seek the life of solitude as an escape from the responsibility of families and relationships, thus misunderstanding both her art and her positive stance toward the nuclear family. In fact to one reader Sarton provides the following advice about not cutting herself off from others: "You imply that what you want is 'love' as a sideline, and 'solitude' as the main current. I don't see this as possible, for love without commitment is pretty cheap. This is where marriage comes in. I read you as terribly afraid of being 'caught' . . . and people who marry simply because they want marriage do often find themselves caught. It looks to me as though you have never loved a man enough to want to marry him, and it's as simple as that. When you do, and I hope you will, there won't be any argument. And then, wouldn't you want children?"[31]

Sarton, who never married, often reflects that she wishes she had children, although her life without these conventional ties seems reasonably complete to most readers and to herself (most of the time). She recognizes that relationships with others cost a great deal of time and pain. She writes in *Recovering* that "passionate love breaks down walls" and that this process can be quite painful: "We are rarely willing to admit how little this initial barrier-breaking is going to count when it comes to the slow, difficult, accepting of each other, when it comes to the irritations and abrasions, and the collisions, too, between two isolated human beings who want to be joined in a lasting relationship. . . .What is never discussed [in a relationship] does not for that reason cease to exist. On the contrary, it may fester and finally become a killing poison."[32] Sexual passion only makes it more difficult for us to achieve agape, what Sarton labels as loving one another "warts and all": "For most of us Eros is an earthquake. There is fear and trembling and, above all, radical change involved. It is quite foolish to deny that our sexuality is deeply disturbing at any age. . . .On the other hand to pretend that

Eros is not a primordial being of the same order as Earth and Chaos is to trivialize or screen off what has to be faced and experienced if we are to come into our humanity as whole beings, and if we are to reach Agape. Perhaps every serious love affair is the reexperiencing of history—psychic history."[33] What Sarton lays out here is the old dictum of knowing thyself. Her candor is reminiscent of the kind of sober self-judgment required of the believer in many passages from the Old and New Testaments. Sarton here models what this kind of intense self-knowledge that comes before sacrificial giving may look like.

One other significant theme of Sarton's work, and perhaps her lasting contribution, is a chronicle of the pains and joys of growing older and the challenges the elderly face in contemporary America. Groundbreaking for her recording of the daily lives, frustrations, and desires of the elderly, Sarton cherishes the aging process even though it brings loss with it. Being older for Sarton means having a greater wealth of knowledge and experience on which to build. She describes her view of old age with a metaphor of an old tree that still flowers and does so richly and remarkably: "But old trees— / The miracle of their flowering / Against the odds— / Bring healing."[34] This sense of endurance comes for Sarton from her earliest age and as a result of her role models (identified earlier in this chapter). In her first memoir, *I Knew a Phoenix,* Sarton attributes her early work in La Gallienne's theater and her friendship with La Gallienne as the two reasons she has learned to endure. She writes that La Gallienne and the theater taught her discipline, drive, and sacrifice: "the sense of what any art demands of its servants, the long discipline of the craft, the devotion, the selflessness, the power to endure."[35] This endurance, initially focused on her art, comes to be focused on her life and her aging, turning elderly life and the recording of it into art.

Sarton's legacy to her readers, both in the form of her writing and in her life as a writer, is indeed a complex one, shaped by her life as a solitary and a lesbian, and yet rewarding for her insights into family life and the legacy of twentieth-century events. Like the picture of the ideal family life Sarton presents through Jane Reid's house in *The Magnificent Spinster* (1985), where home is a safe and nurturing haven from a troubling world and to which Reid pays tribute with fresh flowers, Sarton idealizes the family and seeks that kind of permanent connection. Yet the intensity of her search, and indeed the intensity of her art, causes Sarton ultimately to turn inward, to seek that permanence within her own soul.[36] Therefore Sarton's legacy remains one that also equivocates: it celebrates life within the family from her own position of solitude and idealizes heterosexual love at the same time as she becomes one of the pioneering lesbian authors of her age.

CHAPTER TWO

In Search of Essence
Early Poetry

Sarton invests her eminent talent and energies into poetry with the same desire to live largely in the realm of passion and emotion as that which initially drew her to life in the theater. Sarton's poetic precursors are the lyricists of the 1920s, including Edna St. Vincent Millay (whose sonnets Sarton memorized), Louise Bogan, Elinor Wylie, Ruth Pitter, H. D., and (through his later poetry) William Butler Yeats. Sarton notes later in her life that she turned to formal lyric verse at the very time it was disappearing from the culture, suggesting that this was the reason her poetry did not receive much scholarly attention.

Sarton's embrace of formal lyric poetry has a deep psychological undercurrent. It was not until the late 1940s that Sarton fully accepted her emergent lesbianism and it was not until the early 1960s that she "came out" publicly. Complicated emotions and messy passions linked to her sexuality certainly underlie Sarton's early pain and suffering.[1] Sarton finally achieves wholeness and peace through solitude in the new poems of her 1961 compilation, *Cloud, Stone, Sun, Vine*. These chapters on Sarton's poetry trace this development.

Encounter in April (1937)

Even before the Civic Repertory and the Apprentice Theater which it spawned closed, Sarton had already begun dabbling with writing, remembering through it her love for the women poets of her time and starting several works that would later be revised and included in her publications. When the Apprentice Theater did close, Sarton turned fully to writing, finishing within a year's time both her first novel, *A Single Hound,* and this first volume of poems.

One of the most prominent features of *Encounter in April* is Sarton's early experimentation with the sonnet form in two related sonnet sequences not reproduced in her collected poems. Sarton stresses the worth of poetic form and ties it in with the importance of taking an unflinching look at the realities of love relationships. In an essay entitled "The Writing of a Poem" (initially published in 1957), Sarton presents her theory that form brings reason to bear in shaping emotion.[2]

Sarton's experimentation with the sonnet form in this volume also marks her earliest works, which date back to 1930 when she was seventeen. These early sonnets, many of which become collected in *Encounter in April,* are inspired by Millay's writing, who revived the sonnet form from a careful study of the Elizabethans. In later collections and interviews Sarton rejects all of these early sonnets, however, as early and juvenile, pointing out that she should have studied the Elizabethans directly rather than deriving her models from an intermediary.[3]

Despite Sarton's later rejection of these sonnets, they are to be appreciated for their candor and for their marking the beginning of her exploration of both heterosexual and homosexual love.[4] Susan Sherman identifies the inspiration of the content of these sonnets as being Grace Marie Daley, a woman with whom Sarton had fallen in love in the early 1930s.[5] Sarton may use this experience as the basis of her sonnets, although she hides and/or transforms the genders of her lovers.

In essence these sonnets collected in *Encounters in April* define love, rejecting pious and sentimentalized notions of love for candid descriptions of the trauma and real pain that love, especially gay love, can cause. In chronicling her own experience of love in these sonnets, Sarton refuses to idealize love, and yet at the same time shows the necessity of it as a part of life. Sarton more fully explores this theme of love and pain in her most significant early work, "She Shall Be Called Woman," also published along with some of the early sonnets in *Encounter in April.*

"She Shall Be Called Woman" presents some of the themes that would become characteristic of Sarton, including her exploration of sexual love, the awakening of a woman to the potentials within her own body, and the recasting of mythology in feminist modes. In this poem, a rethinking of the story of Eve from the biblical book Genesis, Sarton maps her desire for autonomy, traces out the emergence of her lesbianism and, more important, her solitude, and participates in the beginnings of rethinking the role of women. Woman's first awakening to her existence, according to the poem, comes in silence and fear. Sarton writes, "She did not cry out / nor move. / She lay quite still."[6] Sarton reiterates this lack of noise or movement in the next stanza—in fact the first action of this newborn is to notice her nakedness and weep.

At heart in this early imagery is the openness of Eve to the violation of Adam because of her innocence and nakedness. She has no choice but to endure his touching and his desire, which cause her pain and fear. Sarton's imagery suggests that Eve learns of her own sexuality only through the violation she receives at the hands of the brute Adam. Eve is neither ready nor able to understand her body and yet through his penetration is forced into experience through pain and confusion. Eve's immediate reaction to Adam's savagery parallels that of many women traumatized by rape: Eve tries to take control of her own suffering by subjecting her hand to pain she can control, thus moving toward the "simpler pain" she later seeks.[7] Sarton depicts through the rest of "She Shall Be Called Woman" Eve's recovery from this first, primal breaking—that is, Eve becomes a recovering rape victim.

In the solitude of the night Eve begins to find some comfort, but the place of comfort is distant; the cry that marks the midpoint of section 2 stresses Eve's desire for rest and the fact that she is unclear as to where this rest will come from. Eve desires peace and seeks oblivion—she wanders into the sea in a symbolic attempt to achieve cleansing, regeneration, and suicide. She finally finds her peace, however, not in denial, nor in "appeasement" or revenge, but rather in learning to understand and take control of herself and her sexuality.

Eve becomes aware of herself and of the changes that have been wrought because of the earlier sexual act. This awareness of the self ends with Eve's reclaiming what is rightfully hers, including her own hand through noting the details of her skin and breasts, and finally in the act of covering her nakedness. Indeed the most erotic portion of this poem is the description of Eve's act of clothing herself, which even suggests masturbation. This exploration leads to Eve's assertion in section 9 that she will never be violated again. In fact she ends by affirming her renewed wholeness, which is both physical and spiritual.

In the final section Eve speaks for the first time, claiming her status as representative of eternal womanhood. Here Eve becomes the symbol of both the tree of life and the tree of the knowledge of good and evil found in Genesis 3. The "seeds" she here mentions allude to the promise of life beginning in her.[8] Eve has, according to Sarton, reinvented herself, finding in herself a new narrative in which she is the beginning and the source of life. The cycles of a woman's life, once thought to connect her to the earth and sin, now become the evidence that she is complete and is symbolically life itself.

The final noteworthy portion of this volume is a series of poems entitled "Landscapes and Portraits," which comprise Sarton's meditation on the relationship between nature and art, a relationship she experienced through her trip to England. The first poem in this section, "On the Atlantic," includes the first mention of solitude in Sarton's published works. Ironically the poet here turns from solitude (and perhaps art itself) to seek love. In "Landscapes and Portraits" England represents for Sarton a permanent, spiritual homeland that anchors the poet even though she has been uprooted numerous times. The conclusion of this sequence shows Sarton turning back to art, revealing the pattern that art gives life meaning and brings both delight and terror with it.

While many of the poems in *Encounter in April* will probably not be considered of lasting greatness, this early volume introduces many of the themes that would come to characterize Sarton's mature work. While Sarton at this early stage had not yet come out of the closet to herself or others, there are many lesbian overtones in this volume. The poem "She Shall Be Called Woman" demonstrates her celebration of the female body as a single, solitary, intact, whole unit. The individual woman who chooses to love (or not) becomes for Sarton the emblem of her own identity and potential.

Inner Landscape (1939)

To turn from *Encounter in April* to *Inner Landscape* is to turn from a poet newly trying her wings to a calmer poet becoming more assured and definite in her vision, despite troubled times. The buildup to World War II in Europe hovers on the fringes of Sarton's art and letters from this time, bringing worry for friends still on the continent and recollections of her and her parents' earlier flight from Belgium. It also leads to a deeper commitment in Sarton to be a poet who lifts the mind from the temporal to the universal. The center of *Inner Landscape* is this goal and it appears most clearly in "Afternoon on Washington Street," where the poet views a tired and desperate world watching the list of atrocities in the headlines. In the midst of this tumult Sarton notices that someone has spoken of past poets—John Milton in particular—as more important and sustaining than modern poets like T. S. Eliot and Ezra Pound, who are involved in the fray. The invocation of Milton challenges Sarton to speak with authority on the power the art of the past has in remaining and in brightening human life. The poet, perhaps with a touch of bravura, thus becomes a modern Milton, ready to lift the mind from material circumstances to the spiritual and eternal.

The other side of this equation is captured in "A Letter to James Stephens." Sarton suggests that Stephens, a contemporary Irish poet Sarton had met through novelist Elizabeth Bowen, had been conducting a search for the pure in poetry that had actually been enacting violence upon nature.[9] She begins by parroting his advice to her to turn away from writing about love and with "chisel" to sculpt something more permanent.[10] Sarton responds by noting how his search for purity is actually cruel and unnatural because it distances him from emotion and sensual experience, leaving him cold and detached. Sarton embraces the search for pure poetry but rejects Stephens's notion that the heart will not lead one there.

"A Letter to James Stephens" marks the beginning of an interest in conversational epistles that will at points come to dominate Sarton's poetry. It also shows Sarton's desire for the spiritual, a quest that will become even more important as she ages. Although Sarton admits that "passion is a frightful thing,"[11] it is her passion that Sarton trusts as a guide. Sarton celebrates passion in the "Canticles," or religious songs, that compose the middle portion of *Inner Landscape*. The centerpiece of this sequence is the sixth canticle, where Sarton offers a meditation on solitude. Essential to Sarton's work is the idea of solitude, even in the midst of love, as a way to truth. True solitude grows from true intimacy, so Sarton thus unites her interest in love with a growing commitment to solitude. Passion becomes for Sarton not an end in itself but a guide to love, truth, and purity.

Canticle 10 returns to the issue of solitude, describing a time when the poet is recovering from a relationship. Representing her spirit as a dove come to rest on a bough, Sarton suggests an initial resistance to solitude, much like the resistance she records in the beginning of *Journal of a Solitude* (1973). Finally, however, solitude embraces the resistant voyager and prepares her for love again.

Thus solitude, like passion, is never an end in itself but a preparation for returning to love. While Sarton returns to the sonnet form again in *Inner Landscape,* the imagery is less raw and more cool, detached, and abstract than that of the earlier volume. In fact Sarton's struggle in these sonnets and in the section entitled "Summary" is rather eloquently summarized in the question at the end of "Memory of Swans," which asks how to arrive at "the purity of a great image freed of its emotion."[12] The quest for pure lyric must take one to the "great image" underneath the emotion that will capture it, thus going beyond the surface to the bedrock of any experience. This movement from surface to substance marks the sonnets and the poems under the section entitled "Summary."

The sonnets of *Inner Landscape* primarily record unrequited love. In the third sonnet Sarton imagines herself bleeding against cold marble that will not even register the stain.[13] She hopes that love for her will renew like nature in the closing couplet of sonnet 6. Sonnet 9 recognizes that, while one can attempt to deny the love one feels, such denial only causes pain. Ultimately sonnet 12 smoothly captures the problem of this sequence through the image of a flower amid nettles. The flower becomes symbolic of the good that comes from love, while the nettles represent the pain often associated with it. Sarton challenges her readers to pick the flower even if they get pricked or stung.[14]

The section "Summary" likewise begins with a problem and searches for the bedrock image underneath. The poet appears cynical about love in the title poem, "Address to the Heart," which shows one of Sarton's darkest images for love: a poison that has infected the sufferer's entire body. The poet searches for peace in solitude after being hurt and it is in the poem "After Silence" that this quest is accomplished. The "great image" here is solitude itself. Like the sonnet's nettle metaphor for love, solitude becomes the medicine to cure the soul when love turns foul.

The nettle symbolizes more than physical love. In the earliest section of *Inner Landscape,* "From the Nettle," art is also figured as a plant with stinging thorns. In "Prayer Before Work" Sarton explores her goals for her art. She calls to the "Great One," praying that her art will have "ease," "precision," and "strict form."[15] Art for Sarton is passion wed to form. Once more the heart is the guide but it is the heart shaped to the rational control of the mind that makes art. In "Architectural Image" Sarton again considers this idea, suggesting that "the structure of [artistic] passion is a spire."[16] This image is reminiscent of Yeats's idea of history as a gyre but sets it on its end.[17] "Granted This World" suggests that art must be set apart and indeed sanctified. And finally in "Landscape" Sarton once again uses a natural metaphor to suggest that the life of the artist must be centered in solitude. Indeed the description of the landscape in this poem very much fits what Sarton eventually chose for herself when she moved to her final home in Maine.

Inner Landscape represents Sarton meditating on the nature of art and love, and beginning to conceive of herself as a serious artist. She suggests here that art is the highest good for her and it becomes the central purpose of her life. Solitude becomes vital to this idea and the poet herself begins to accept a lifestyle characterized by inner growth and meditation.

The Lion and the Rose (1948)

The beginning sections of *The Lion and the Rose* allow the reader to see Sarton at her strongest and most characteristic. Her vision and assertiveness perhaps become clearest in this volume because at this time she personally comes into her glory as a traveling and presenting American poet and through finding a lifelong relationship with Matlack, while in New Mexico. In this volume Sarton discovers the liberating vision of digging deep into the landscape of her heart in search of the bedrock image that will provide love and meaning. Once more the central themes of solitude and the chronicling of daily experience appear, but they now are central and vividly American.

IN SEARCH OF ESSENCE

Much of the poetry in the first two sections of this volume derives from Sarton's 1940–1941 travels throughout the United States as a reading poet. In letters dating from these trips, as well as in the poetry itself, Sarton becomes fully concerned with America. Until this point in her work Sarton's eyes were always cast nostalgically back to Europe. While touring America in the early 1940s Sarton begins to hear the voices of America and experience its unique heritage.[18]

A letter dated 27 October 1940, addressed to her friend Polly Thayer Starr, provides insights into Sarton's turn toward America and its impact on her creative processes. Sarton reflects here on a visit to Winchester, Virginia (which inspires a poem of the same title): "You suddenly come to a town like Winchester, Va. . . . [with] memories of battles ringing in the air—(That town changed hands 72 times in the Civil War.) As a northerner in the South, I am filled with shame. If ever anything proved the wrongs of passion, even a passion for justice . . . the war between the states certainly did . . . We attacked the problem without ever trying to answer it, destroyed all possibility of its being answered with justice."[19] Sarton here begins to identify herself as fully American: she describes herself as a northerner and embraces a collective "we" in relation to this period of American history.

In describing the process of moving from experience to the writing of poems based on that experience, Sarton offers the key that unites this letter and the art she creates. In *Writings on Writing* (1980) Sarton echoes William Wordsworth in her embracing of the quiet after an event and using the remembrance of that event as the source of poetry. "That explosion is now over," Sarton explains. "The moment when the writing of a poem begins is a moment of high excitement, but of an entirely different kind to the experiencing of its birth as an idea for a poem."[20] For Sarton poems come as single ideas and individual lines that are then given flesh by the conscious mind of the poet: "It has been my experience . . . that a single line floats up into consciousness. . . . This line very often . . . suggests the kind of musical stir the poem is to make, suggests the time, sometimes even the form."[21] Then the poet takes that line, abstracts the sound and the form from it, and thus shapes the poem by conscious reasoning out of the ideas offered by the subconscious.[22]

The kernel of the idea for her poem on Winchester, Va., is found in the October 1940 letter to Starr and centers on the idea that the past is still living there. Sarton shifts the emphasis between the poem and the letter: In the letter the past brings shame to the northern observer for the war and the evils of Reconstruction. In the poem, however, the past becomes a source of nurturing. Sarton suggests in the poem that the war has died—in the letter, it lives on in the shame of the viewer and the issues facing the town—however the past is not fully resolved, for history is felt in the streets of Winchester. Sarton's reflections in the poem thus grow from a contemplation of her experience and are then shaped into art by form, memory, and reason.[23]

This chronicling of experience and the power of memory, both personal and cultural, as a source and corrective surfaces in Sarton's most famous poem, "My Sisters, O My Sisters." Here Sarton captures the themes and sacrifices that make up a writer's life in general and a woman writer's life in particular. In the first section of "My Sisters," years before this kind of search became fashionable, Sarton takes the reader on a spiritual journey through women's history, cataloging the greatness and cost of women's art. This chronicle is meant to respond to the other impetus of this poem, a 1925 poem by Sara Teasdale entitled "The Sisters." In a 1990 interview with David Bradt, Sarton labels Teasdale's verse "sentimental," a characteristic she maintains better writers like Yeats eventually reject.[24] Teasdale's poem concludes that no previous woman writer offers an acceptable model or tradition;[25] Sarton, though, responds that it is not in the spoken words of historical women writers but in their silences that contemporary women writers can find a source and tradition for their art.

Sarton's journey begins with Dorothy Wordsworth, who was "too busy" with her own thoughts on her deathbed to want to read. Sarton hypothesizes that women who want to write "are strange monsters who renounce the treasure / Of their silence for a curious devouring pleasure."[26] Dorothy Wordsworth becomes the counter example, being a woman who sought her silences in the end. Sarton then catalogs what the women who chose to pursue writing cost themselves and others. She lists Emily Dickinson, Christina Rossetti, Sappho, George Sand, and others who gave up their fulfillment— and ultimately their lives—for the sake of art.

After this despairing list of examples Sarton turns the tables and suggests that this sacrifice results from society, which makes it virtually impossible for an artistic woman to do otherwise. In her list Sarton suggests that the intensity of women's art costs women more than it does men and ultimately does not even aid them. While optimistic that one day women will be able to write and become more fully human, without having to renounce other aspects of life, Sarton concedes that this state has not yet come about.

This theme of the necessity of renunciation in women's art surfaces consistently throughout Sarton's work. In a 1977 interview

Sarton reflects on this theme again, pinpointing the central idea of "My Sisters": the rejection of heterosexual marriage as then practiced (an idea she dislikes acknowledging). Sarton here recalls the sacrifices women artists must make to be artists at all: "I think it's very hard for a woman to be married and have children and be a first-rate artist. If you try to think of the first-rate artists who are women, practically none of them have married and have had children."[27] Although Sarton suggests that this situation is beginning to change, her rejection of heterosexual marriage and family for the female artist remains a touchy undercurrent especially for her in her work.

The next section of "My Sisters" searches for a place in which to ground women's art and finds it in women's ability to nourish and love others. Sarton calls upon women to remember their ideals, including their desire for love and their nascent powers to love; to grow and nurture, whether it be flowers or children; and to embrace and rely on their own innate wisdom—a wisdom Sarton conceives of as both dove and serpent, thus uniting both sweetness and cunning.

In the third section of "My Sisters" Sarton returns to her catalog, this time situating women between Eve and Mary and deconstructing the virgin/whore dichotomy which has haunted Western women. Rather than accepting them as separate entities, Sarton suggests that Eve and Mary are two sides in the one heart of women. Eve represents for Sarton knowledge and wisdom (often hidden by men) and Mary represents the eternal mother, nurturing and loving. Hell for women comes from a lack of balance between these two aspects. Sarton suggests that some areas of imbalance occur in marriage where women give up power because of bad choices made in confusion. Rather, Sarton urges, they need to seek their spiritual source.

IN SEARCH OF ESSENCE

The final passage of "My Sisters" exhorts women to reconnect to the earth and to their deepest passions. Years before Mary Daly's revolutionary revisions of patriarchal religion, Sarton suggests that many women have lost this primal connection. The pathway back to truth and wholeness for women, Sarton maintains, is reconnecting with their spiritual beings. Long before the revolutionary thought of *Women's Ways of Knowing* and long before the call for traditionally feminine virtues to come into the public sphere, a call set forth by Carolyn Heilbrun, Sandra M. Gilbert, Susan Gubar, and others, Sarton issues the call and envisions its utopian outcomes. In the final stanza Sarton argues that women have betrayed themselves by allowing men to usurp the role of creator. To halt this usurpation, she entreats, the god of passion must be called back and women must reclaim their power.

Sarton's beautiful evocation of this dream in "My Sisters" is neither sentimental nor weak. *The Lion and the Rose* represents Sarton herself coming into full balance as a woman and poet. It presents a clear, complex, and holistic vision for a new, matriarchal tomorrow, empowering both men and women—a vision also lived out in her best fiction and memoirs.

The Leaves of the Tree (1950) and *The Land of Silence* (1953)

When we come to *The Leaves of the Tree* and *The Land of Silence* we find Sarton contemplating nature and spirituality.[28] "The First Autumn," a poem written in memory of her mother, looks to the natural world as a site of renewal, even for those who have died. "Letter from Chicago," the poem Sarton wrote to celebrate Virginia

Woolf's life and to come to terms with her suicide, brings out this interest fully, linking Woolf with the cycles of nature and suggesting that Woolf's art survives her death. Here again Sarton locates her own creativity in the heritage of women writers of the past. Gilbert and Gubar argue that Sarton's poem in honor of Woolf represents a transcendence of time that is ultimately necessary and "redemptive" for women writers.[29] Yet this poem also suggests, as do most works in these volumes, that a woman writer should seek a spiritual or natural rhythm that is more than the mere passage of years.[30]

Sarton naturalizes religion in the poetry of these volumes, suggesting that orthodox religion is not beneficial for the writer. Instead she suggests, along with Simone Weil, that nature provides the truths sought by a writer. As shown in a 1977 interview, Sarton often quotes Weil's definition of prayer and then connects it to the writing of poetry: "'Absolute attention is prayer.' Of course, you can't write a poem without absolute attention."[31] This religious focus has led critics such as Stephen Robitaille to suggest that Sarton is following Zen Buddhism in her ideas, but even this designation fails to convey the entirety of Sarton's vision.[32] Sarton is not Christian, or at least if she is so it is only a very broad, unorthodox sense. Certainly her ennoblement of solitude, appreciation of nature, and dedication to sacramental living are imbued with what Richard J. Foster calls the "Immanent tradition" in Christian practice.[33] However Sarton rejects any organized religion and embraces nature and nature's rhythms at the same time that her writing teaches valuable lessons to any adherents of the world's orthodox faiths.

Readers can see this rejection of organized religion and the invocation of another form of spirituality by pairing her poems

"Myth" and "The Seas of Wheat." "Myth" suggests that static human creations and organizations for containing God fail to recognize, and indeed deny, God's power. The poem centers on a temple about which humans are proud—until the gods show their power by destroying it. Those who invested themselves in this temple and the religion it represents are liberated when they learn to observe in silence, stillness, and with awe the power and majesty of the gods and their uncontrollable (and unpredictable) nature.

Sarton takes religion and religious language out of the temple in "Myth" and invests it back into nature in "The Seas of Wheat." This poem is imbued with the language of Catholicism, crediting nature with the transforming power denied the temple in the earlier poem. Sarton invests the wheat in the field with the power of the religious sacrament of the Eucharist. The wheat becomes the symbol (through the seed dying to be reborn as wheat) of Christ even before it is made into the communion bread. For Sarton the transubstantiation occurs in the poem as the wheat's growth from green plant to harvest to nourishment. Thus any moment during which bread is made and served becomes religious in its significance as Sarton moves from an orthodox Christian position to a more pantheist cosmology in which we are one with the cyclical power of nature. In the end what is most important to Sarton is not religion but the intensity that leads to poetic expression.

As Kenneth Burke points out in his study of religious language, this moving of the religious into the natural transforms the natural world into a religion.[34] Sarton's art enacts this natural spirituality. Her poem "The Tree" walks the thin line between a natural mysticism and an intense but orthodox religiosity, such as one can find in the poetry of George Herbert. The poem could be read as a powerful meditation on the relationship between the Christ child and the cross as symbolized by the child and the tree. More appropriate to Sarton, however, is the idea that the tree itself is holy and the connection between the child and tree that occurs at Christmas brings the natural, and thereby spiritual, indoors.

Drawing on Weil's idea of prayerlike attention, Sarton's "Of Prayer" explores the intense contemplation of the natural as a spiritual process. This poem, addressed to God as Sarton understands God, begins by rejecting what most people would characterize as prayer. Prayer for Sarton occurs not in formal ritual but during instances when we are not even thinking of God, as in moments of passionate love or during the creation of art. Sarton suggests that it is erroneous to think that God is concerned with orthodox religious forms. Rather God is best pleased by the life well lived, which is the ideal prayer for Sarton.[35]

Thus Sarton enacts what Renée Curry rightly labels a revision of the meditative tradition. Curry writes that Sarton and poet Elizabeth Bishop "engage and simultaneously reform the meditative tradition, but they do it in radically charged, culturally revolutionary ways."[36] Curry goes on to suggest that both writers thus "renew and make change, but they also make their mark as revisionists by that which seems profoundly significant to the original idea or form."[37] Sarton indeed makes nature spiritual and her poetry becomes a site where both the orthodox and unorthodox of any faith can feel at home. This natural spirituality, akin to the transcendentalist ideals of Ralph Waldo Emerson and Henry David Thoreau but invested deeply in emerging feminist practices, becomes for Sarton the arena of truth. While not nearly as certain or free of change as organized religious tradition, it is nonetheless pure and nurturing.

IN SEARCH OF ESSENCE

In Time Like Air (1958)

In the title poem of her 1958 volume *In Time Like Air* Sarton asks how the soul matures. Her defining image concerns salt, which dissolves in water and reemerges in air. Sarton asks what elements have the same effects on the soul that water and air have on salt; this question and its answer frame the central themes of this volume. Sarton's immediate response within the poem is that love dissolves the soul and an attitude of detachment causes it to reform.

In the poem "Where Dream Begins" Sarton directs the reader where to find spiritual wealth regardless of outward circumstances. Love combined with detachment becomes the answer, connecting Sarton once more to the meditative tradition. The fulfillment of dreams and the realization of truth are associated with a honeycomb, an image of intense, orgiastic sweetness often associated with triumphant women writers.[38] In all the poems of this collection—and particularly in the nature poems—Sarton probes deeply and honestly, developing works that are more open and discursive and less didactic than her earlier writings.

In "The Frog, That Naked Creature" Sarton turns the frog's nakedness and vulnerability into positive attributes that she wants to emulate. Openness to joys and trials becomes the hallmark of a soul seeking growth. Yet this openness also becomes symbolic of both the pain that leads to growth and the faith of the poet in natural processes. While nature and circumstance can shake the poet to her foundation, Sarton learns that perhaps this shaking is best after all. The frog thus teaches the poet to surrender hubris for humiliation, a choice that leads to maturity.

"The Phoenix" shows the other side of this spiritual situation.

Like "The Furies," which depicts someone who accommodates the darkness, "The Phoenix" shows the dangers of fleeing and thus not nurturing oneself and others through love and detachment. Sarton returns to this icon of the phoenix again and again throughout her writing as a strong supportive myth of the rebirth she wants to experience. "The Phoenix" presents the first appearance of this image in Sarton's poetry. Ironically, however, Sarton here sees the phoenix as a symbol of an emotionally battering anger, though nevertheless a force which could offer the potential for growth—if not reacted to by fear and flight. Only later does this bird that rises from its own ashes become the central symbol Sarton uses for herself. In this poem the bird awakens the speaker to the chaos and darkness in herself that she would prefer not to acknowledge. Rather than learning through desire and the dark night of the soul, so her soul can grow spiritually, the speaker instead expends more energy pushing growth away and denying it.

After the fifth stanza, though, the perspective of the poem changes. Although the poet feels sympathy toward the speaker's fear, she notes that the phoenix is an angel in disguise. Years before the call for women to tap into their rage—an idea of particular prominence in 1980s feminism—Sarton asks women to accept their anger and probe it for the truths it offers. Sarton hopes the rejected phoenix representing this anger will return with its empowering message. By rejecting the bird, the symbol of her own anger, the speaker of the poem rejects growth and wholeness.

Sarton continues to return in this volume to a reliance on nature for spiritual insight. In "At Muzot" Sarton refers to the earth itself as "sacramental" and in "Nativity" she uses Gerard Manley Hopkins's term "inscape" (the energy a poet invests in nature and art) to suggest a religious reverence for Mother Earth.[39] In "Mediterranean" Sarton defines this reverence as the essence of prayer.

"At Muzot" celebrates the idea of sacramental nature. Sarton refers in this poem to one important poetic predecessor, Rainer Maria Rilke, whose use of nature parallels her own. Muzot is the place where Rilke wrote some of his most famous works, including his *Sonnets to Orpheus*, which were composed "after a terrible long silence."[40] Her admiration of Rilke informs the entire volume of *In Time Like Air*.

"At Muzot" answers the question posed in the title poem, "In Time Like Air." The virtue of detachment becomes realized in the vision of Rilke that Sarton sees at his Muzot home. Sarton does not contradict her earlier observations on intense passionate engagement as the beginning of truth—rather she suggests that true detachment is the result of intense engagement with life. The temporal and the divine become incarnate in the poet through her interaction with nature.

Cloud, Stone, Sun, Vine (1961)

"At Muzot" becomes the bridge between the volumes *In Time Like Air* and *Cloud, Stone, Sun, Vine:* the title of the later volume is taken from a line of this poem. Cloud, stone, sun, and vine represent elements that take on spiritual meaning for Sarton and through which she is able to make contact with God; the poet discovers holiness and the "essence" of things as time flows like air. As Sarton seeks greater detachment, she begins to embrace solitude as more and more of a necessity for spiritual growth. Together the poems in these two volumes lay the groundwork for the early journals, where she articulates the solitary life that characterizes much of her appeal as an early feminist and as a guide to others.

Most of the poems published in *Cloud, Stone, Sun, Vine* are reprints, taken from all the previous volumes except her earliest, *Encounter in April*—only the last section entitled "New Poems" has in it new works. The majority of this section contains a sonnet sequence, "A Divorce of Lovers," which is followed by seven short lyric poems.

In the sequence "A Divorce of Lovers" Sarton sets as her theme the problem of form. She does this through a question, appearing at the end of sonnet 1, that asks if "Reason" can make art grow out of this separation between lovers.[41] The emotions described in this poem are evidently still raw and painful. In a letter to Sarton, in fact, Louise Bogan complains that this sonnet sequence is too obviously about a lesbian affair and that the ending is too neat.[42] Despite Bogan's critique, though, the sequence reveals a central tenet of Sarton's thought. Sarton here demonstrates how a mastery of emotion by reason can lead to universal insights into the end of relationships—insights that can transcend the occasion and give rise to poetry.

The rest of the poetry in the "New Poems" section explore the nature of the wisdom solitude brings, and begin the kind of detailed chronicle of the ebb and flow of Sarton's life that finds its most eloquent expression in her journals. It is no wonder that her most famous memoir, *Journal of a Solitude,* which unveils her discovery of a writing style that captures daily life, and her most successful novel, *Mrs. Stevens Hears the Mermaids Singing,* are contemporary to Sarton's creation of lyric poetry celebrating solitude.

It is here that Sarton also shifts her language of love from the physical and sexual love explored in the sonnets to a metaphysical love. This spiritual love, though, is richly evoked by the same sexually charged language she used earlier, much like the language of many of the great mystic writers of the Western world.

Thus *Cloud, Stone, Sun, Vine* finds a mature and aging Sarton discovering and adapting to the life of a solitary artist. Although love relationships still figure in Sarton's life, this volume finds her fully articulating the relationship between love, art, and solitude, and contains in "A Divorce of Lovers" her strongest sonnets to date. Sarton republishes her older poetry as a context for the newest, thus presenting for the first time the image of herself that readers had come to love and expect as early as the 1960s. The poetry brings the reader to the brink of Sarton's fullest acceptance of herself as both a lesbian and a solitary—the two sides of Sarton most thoroughly explored, respectively, in *Mrs. Stevens Hears the Mermaids Singing* and *Journal of a Solitude.*

A Private Mythology (1966)

A Private Mythology chronicles a spiritual pilgrimage Sarton makes at the age of fifty. It continues the exploration begun in the previous volume and deepens into a full-fledged religious statement. In these poems Sarton turns to the ancient religions of Japan, India, and Greece for perspectives and meaning other than what she finds in America and Europe, conducting a search that proves profound both for its pain and its insights.[43]

Sarton starts this journey at the farthest remove from the West, both geographically and culturally, in her travels to Japan. Yet Sarton characterizes this journey to Japan as a homecoming, breaking down the distances and distinctions. In "A Child's Japan" Sarton suggests that the rhythms of her childhood are akin to what she expects to see in Japan. She conceives of her father being like a Buddhist monk in his study, intense in his meditations for hours; her mother she sees as fostering in the family a simple style, which further demonstrates for Sarton how much she believes her family had in common with the Japanese. Going to Japan is thus like a return to Sarton's roots as well as a spiritual quest abroad.

The poetry itself takes on a simplified style, perhaps inspired by Japan. Sarton's lines are shorter, the words and images more concrete and precise. As she relates her experiences in Japan, the verse embodies the clarity and simplicity of traditional Japanese art. Sarton characterizes this austerity of style as a type of violence, but as evidenced in "Second Thoughts on the Abstract Gardens of Japan," a violence seen as necessary. For Sarton it is violent because it is a whittling down and erasing of the inessential on the quest for refining the self. This violence is painful for both the servant met by the poet ("An Exchange of Gifts") and for the poet herself ("Lake Chuzen-ji"). Ultimately, as Sarton concludes in "Wood, Paper, Stone," this violence characterizes the most Japanese of poetic forms, the haiku.

Some of Sarton's poems in this volume, particularly those collected under "Japanese Prints," adapt the haiku form. Proper haiku form consists of three lines containing, respectively, five, seven, and five syllables. Sarton manipulates this form, keeping its condensed style and intense look at specific natural detail, but reducing it even further and suggesting in selections like "Four Views of Fujiyama" and "Tourist" that even the haiku may be too elaborate. Sarton here sets for herself the task of writing even more compressed lines than the traditional Japanese form dictates.

IN SEARCH OF ESSENCE

Sarton's interest in Japan eventually turns to the lives of women and the renewing power of ritual. Her Japanese companion and translator, Kyoko, figures in several of these poems. It is through Kyoko that Sarton realizes her own Western detachment and comes to seek something more akin to Eastern mysticism. In "Kyoko," Kyoko shows Sarton the Western world refracted through Eastern eyes. In "An Exchange of Gifts" Kyoko facilitates Sarton's encounter with a servant woman, which leads to another change in Sarton's perceptions. Sarton's request for the name of this servant surprises the servant, leaving Sarton to reflect that she has observed life so far only with a detached interest. The servant, Eiko, who returns Sarton's gift of words with a precious and fragile decorated fan, breaks this barrier between Sarton and the world, suggesting to her a way for the poet to enter experience more fully.

In "Wood, Paper, Stone" Sarton probes this new mode of existence and creates for the reader her experience of this perceptual change. In section 4 of this poem, in a series of three statements beginning with "so," Sarton enacts this new awareness. She equates a Japanese person's awe before some stones to a Frenchman's quotation of Mallarmé; she enters into the essence of a moment where Kyoko smiles at her; and she senses an almost primal energy in natural wood. The conclusion of this change of perception emerges in "Second Thoughts on the Abstract Gardens of Japan," which portrays Sarton's return to Japan via memory. She ponders what it means to embrace the violence of this simplicity that leads to an intimate living-in-the-moment, and hopes that this constant, intense awareness finds its expression in her art.

Sarton's description of her trip to India continues the journalistic quality marking much of her travel poetry in *A Private Mythology*.

At first she observes that she does not feel completely at home in India. When arriving in Calcutta she feels fear; consequently the images in "The Approach—Calcutta" suggest stagnation and death. The gods of India, ancient and dominantly male, overwhelm her and seem to be embroiled in some dire cosmic battle. In "Notes from India" she stresses that even a ritual cleansing is performed in polluted water. In part one of "Notes from India," though, Sarton realizes once more the lesson about Western detachment that she earlier sketched: she describes a fall that allows her to come into more physical contact with India. Although detachment is still a key element in Sarton's writing and revising of poetry, her approach to life seeks now to discard as much as possible the Western "camera eye" and replace it with being really and fully in touch.[44]

Perhaps the fullness of this new involvement with experience reaches its most startling outcome during her trip to Greece and, through this, in her haunting poem "At Delphi." When visiting Greece in "Birthday on the Acropolis" Sarton is shocked by Western order and regimented architecture, symbolically representing the West itself since Greece is the birthplace of Western thought and its "camera eye." In "Nostalgia for India" Sarton misses the confusion of life in the East and its candid expression of pain and pleasure. She prays to Pallas Athena in "Birthday on the Acropolis" not for wisdom but for strength and stamina.[45] "At Delphi," though, most fully expresses the darkness Sarton sees at the center of Western thought as she turns her newfound perceptions back onto Western detachment.

The landscape of "At Delphi" is harsh and threatening. Words are not clear and pure, but open to multiple meanings and ambiguity, and the universe demands attention of everyone but grants no answers. Sarton concludes that all of us face these fears and realities alone. But her most dire conclusions come in the clarity and enigma of the final five lines of the poem.

Sarton's portrait of St. John the Revelator in this series of Greek poems provides a key to understanding the full import of these final lines of "At Delphi." St. John becomes a figure of both exile and illumination, being awarded the gift of prophecy and being overpowered by revelation. "On Patmos" depicts him as alone and in ecstasy, finding truth through his solitude. The second part of Sarton's "Ballads of the Traveler" suggests that the angels who brought prophecy to St. John nearly drove him mad and that the only way for him to keep his sanity was to silence them by writing. This depiction harkens back to Sarton's earlier presentation of forces she labels furies, as can be found in the volume *In Time Like Air* in such poems as "Islands and Wells," "The Furies," and "The Frog, That Naked Creature."[46] These dark forces are maddening, pushing the poet toward death, but may in the end offer salvation.

What Sarton ultimately finds in her trips to Japan, India, and Greece is a new mode of being. According to her new understanding, to experience life with a "camera eye" and uncritically adopt Western modes of thought and being means to commodify, exploit, and violate. To fully embrace experience—to fall to the earth (as suggested in "Notes from India")—becomes Sarton's newest spiritual goal. This new awareness revolutionizes her poetic expression, making it the more direct, visceral, and crystalline form found in the poetry of *A Private Mythology,* such as in the animal poems of section 3 and more indirectly in the elegies of section 4. Although Sarton does return to the West she now perceives her detachment as being useful for writing but ultimately wrong for living.

CHAPTER THREE

The Sage Emerges
Later Poetry

As Does New Hampshire (1967)

In this volume we again encounter, as in *Cloud, Stone, Sun, Vine*, a retrospective of Sarton's poetry, collected and republished. The seven new poems in this volume continue the expression of Sarton's increasing spiritual depth and her rejection of Western modes of being (first presented in *A Private Mythology*). In "A Glass of Water" Sarton offers an implied comparison between chlorinated, purified city water and the country water of the well. Sarton prefers the water that retains traces of and a connection to the earth. This water, like the act of providing detailed attention to nature, offers renewal and refreshment.

The New Hampshire landscape Sarton here depicts is natural and fairly uninvolved with human life (other than with the poet herself). The two poems that end the collection, "Stone Walls" and "A Guest," explore this natural landscape and the results of humans entering it. Sarton sees people as having some interaction with and control over nature. In "March-Mad," for instance, Sarton finds lushness through contemplating the seed catalog and deciding what she will plant in the following spring to enhance the natural. The stone walls in the poem of that title symbolize this interaction between humans and nature. The walls chart the eternal struggle of humanity trying to subdue nature. Farmers fight with the land, Sarton writes, to achieve some sort of victory through the erection of walls and the possession of land that once was wild. Then war comes and destroys all of this labor. Sarton suggests, though, that war leads people to become more resilient and she admires this burgeoning strength.

Sarton identifies herself as made from the marriage of England and Belgium, two countries well acquainted with war. She views industrial society as the recognition of farmers and others that they cannot contain the land's power. She rejects these societies, the walls they build and the wars they wage, along with the Western individualism they represent, in favor of a purer, more natural relationship with nature. The tamed and leveled pastures, Sarton maintains, have lost their memory and have been deprived of their soul, perhaps irrevocably so.

"A Guest" finishes the query begun in "Stone Walls," suggesting that our valuing of growth and progress is sorely amiss and that we rid nature of its beauty and integrity in order to achieve these aims. Sarton watches the animals around her home in New Hampshire, seeing herself as a disturbance to their natural cycle. She recognizes, however, that she is certainly not the dominant ruler of this land and these animals, both of which follow other rules. The reference to ash cans in her description of herself is at least partially a humorous disparagement of her own lifelong habit of smoking. Sarton tries to find her place in this natural world but discovers instead that each animal and person is its own entity, entire and individuated, though also connected to the rhythms of this natural life. She is exhilarated and humbled by this realization. Nature thus calls into question and undercuts Western acquisitiveness.

When another person arrives in this natural setting Sarton views this other as an outsider. Her final couplet completes the realignment of values, suggesting that people are the wild ones and that animals are already tamed in the rules and laws of their environment. Animals reside in natural harmony; humans abuse this harmony and perhaps inflict even greater harm by taming the tamed.

In these seven poems Sarton takes the stance of a prophetic sage, suggesting the need for us to rethink our values. This reevaluation begins with the epiphanies she experienced in Japan and India—epiphanies that were first described in *A Private Mythology,* then brought to bear on Greece, and at last realized more fully in these New Hampshire poems. In age and wisdom Sarton begins to model for others the life she hopes they will pursue: a life in harmony with the natural, in touch with simplicity and solitude, and in favor of a fundamental rejection of Western values such as ambition, individualism, and progress, which seek to contain and tame nature rather than adapt harmoniously to it.

A Grain of Mustard Seed (1971)

Sarton's ninth volume of poetry takes a clear and unremitting look at the state of America in the turbulent 1960s. The reader experiences a sense of the problems' depths and of hope through the possibility of human empathy and compassion. The faith alluded to by the biblical reference in the title is a faith in this human potential to overcome darkness and seek light. In "A Last Word" Sarton describes the sixties as an era of darkness but presents it as something to be struggled against. The obstacles, however, seem profound: the battle for civil rights and the problems of facing desegregation ("Ballad of the Sixties" and "The Ballad of Ruby"), the turmoil at Kent State ("We'll to the Woods No More, The Laurels are Cut Down"), and the continuing dark legacy of the Holocaust (part 3 of "The Invocation to Kali"). Through it all Sarton hopes these are merely growing pains that will eventually lead to peace.

Sarton's most succinct statement of the hope and darkness of the sixties, and her own sustaining if unorthodox faith, comes in the poem "Easter, 1968," which begins by suggesting in its series of three "Now" statements that Jesus Christ is still suffering for humankind. Sarton posits that Christ's crucifixion should lead every one of his followers into a deep self-contemplation because all bear responsibility for Christ's suffering. In a series of balancing ideas the reader sees how Christ's hunger derives from our greed, his thirst from our laziness, and his injury from our lack of love and care for one another. Sarton concludes that the truth to be found here is that our peace is dependant on caring for others. Again she affirms the practice of self-reflection not for its own sake but as preparation for better service to others.

The second stanza suggests dual meanings through the figure of the suffering African. In one sense Sarton may be again referring to Christ, who was from that portion of the world and is often depicted as having dark skin. In a second (and perhaps more significant) sense Sarton suggests that the African oppressed in America is a representation of the suffering Christ. This second reading is supported by other poems in this collection. Sarton presents the African's plight as something that needs to be examined again, implying the need for Americans to atone for the cruelty of the past. By recalling his plight we can hear with broken hearts the words of Christ through the African, perhaps enabling us to resolve the problems of racism and the lingering legacy of slavery in the South, and find peace through love and care of others.

Sarton's ethic of compassion also surfaces strongly in her

explorations of the plight of the aged in American society. The poems on this subject in this volume mark the beginning of one of Sarton's greatest later themes, which finds its fullest expression in her later journals. Sarton admires the elderly in poems such as "For Rosalind on Her Seventy-fifth Birthday." She also recognizes that aging and illness are often companions, hoping that the patients in "Night Watch" will recover, or at least not suffer the indignities she describes in "A Hard Death." Hope for this turbulent era comes in the form of compassion for the aged and the dying.

Apparently absent from Sarton's portrait of the sixties is the struggle for women's rights. Although a pioneer feminist in this struggle, she often rejects the move away from the family and domesticity that many feminists of the time embrace. Despite her disavowal of this characteristic of feminism, Sarton's call for compassion and her focus on political engagement actually further necessary feminist initiatives and reform.

Sarton's feminism surfaces in part in her meditations entitled "The Invocation to Kali" and "The Muse as Medusa." Both mythological figures represent the dark side of the female. Sarton suggests that they also can represent the destruction that is necessary before change and rebirth can occur. In "Invocation" Sarton embodies the terror and uncertainty of her age in the figure of Kali, the goddess who births all things out of darkness and violence. Looking squarely at the darkness within human nature and human fate, Sarton resists easy and useless platitudes. The first part of "Invocation" wrestles with questions about how to live with and overcome this violence. She argues that poetry too has the potential to cry out against the violence and therefore finds its source in Kali also. The invocation seeks to atone for ignoring and forgetting about the violence, for Sarton claims that until it is acknowledged nothing new will be born.

Part 3 of "Invocation" turns to the specter of the Holocaust, wondering why people so easily forget and in so doing potentially repeat this horror. Sarton writes that in such mass horrors one at best cannot see God's providential work and at worst comes to believe that God is not there at all. Instead we become sated with material possessions, ignoring the taints they may carry. Sarton concludes in part 4 that we must recognize and understand these horrific events and that Kali must be acknowledged before we can recover.

The violence Sarton accepts as a necessary part of creation, like the violence of childbirth, comes to be seen in her description of the woman artist and her muse in "The Muse as Medusa." The image of birth and embryonic fluid becomes embodied in Sarton's depiction of the poet, and what the poet emerges into is love, like a wanted baby. Sarton sees Medusa's cave as a warm and nurturing place.[1] Through facing Medusa's stony gaze the artist is made whole by seeing the deepest parts of herself.

Sarton's clear, cold look at women's selfhood and creativity aligns her deeply with the feminist movement of the late 1960s and early 1970s. She acknowledges the whole range of women's experience, from anger to healing love, and validates it for her reader. Even her deceptively simple poem honoring Renaissance painter Pieter de Hooch, "Dutch Interior," becomes an evocation of universal womanhood. Sarton celebrates the hard-won serenity of a moment in de Hooch's painting that depicts a woman calmly sewing. She sees here the limits of de Hooch's masculine vision, suggesting that what he does not depict is the turmoil that has been subdued by this woman's heart and will. Margot Peters identifies the woman in the center of this poem as one of Sarton's lovers, a "'fire engine' of a woman," Baroness Hannie Van Till.[2] But the mastery of this poem is that Sarton shapes her own turbulent and painful love affairs into a celebration and validation of women's creativity, art, and love, and sees in these ideals salvation for the chaos of her age.

A Durable Fire (1972)

In the most famous poem of this collection, "Gestalt at Sixty," Sarton exposes the less-than-ideal side of solitude. By the early 1970s, because of works like *Plant Dreaming Deep* (1968), Sarton had a following that included at least some misguided fans who romanticized Sarton's solitary life. Always aware of the pain of solitude as well as its joys, Sarton sets out in "Gestalt" to give the fullest picture she can of the solitary life.

Part 1 of "Gestalt" recounts the initial turmoil that infected Sarton's life when she first sought solitude. When she came to her new home ten years before she found that nature itself seemed out-of-tune with her, as though she and nature were only joined together by torture. In her early days there she often awoke with fear and panic, afraid of dying alone or of something happening to the house. Solitude for Sarton, while a deep well of inspiration, becomes on occasion far from ideal. Sarton writes that solitude brings the past and its pains constantly to mind and that it causes one to obsess about every passing incident. The person in solitude has more time to brood on problems and thus can even begin to see problems as disproportionately larger than a less solitary person might.

THE SAGE EMERGES

Despite solitude's clear drawbacks, Sarton relates that there are ways to deal with these liabilities. She finds that some of these solutions include working out one's anger and feelings in the garden, learning through an open, humble heart the ongoing lessons that solitude and creativity teach, and constantly reminding oneself that one is working toward creating a happier world. This new world emerges through essential lessons, including those of open-mindedness, hope, patience, and self-trust. Sarton thus suggests that, with the correct attitude, solitude can be beneficial.

Sarton then considers how the home of a modern solitary appears to others. Although the reader may assume from Sarton's other writings that her house is detached and isolated from the world, in fact Sarton receives a stream of letters daily and remains fully aware of each day's news. The past remains vital in both its pains and joys, and this past includes love affairs now over. Finally Sarton suggests that all objects, ideas, and people visiting her home change her in some way just as she changes them. The exciting yet terrifying potential Sarton here sees shows that the solitary person is far from being ideally situated in a recreated Garden of Eden.

Ultimately solitude allows Sarton to embrace fully and freely all the richness of life. Virginia Woolf describes in *A Room of One's Own* the creative and androgynous mind as "resonant and porous" and observes "that it transmits emotion without impediment; [is] incandescent, and undivided."[3] Sarton seeks and develops these attributes in her mind through solitude. She writes that she has learned to remain open and vulnerable to every emotion without needing to repress her feelings. She also feels as she ages that she is able to achieve wisdom even in the midst of an increasing weakness and fragility. The cycles of nature enrich her life as she observes them in infinite detail. And, finally, she is beginning to understand and accept death even though she is not yet ready to die.

"Gestalt at Sixty" concludes with a sober but joyous prayer of thanks to God for the richness of solitude. Long before the idea of the gratitude journal, first developed by Sarah Ban Breathnach[4] and then popularized by Oprah Winfrey, came into national prominence, Sarton models gratitude-journal writing in many of her poems and prayers (and in her journals themselves). The closing prayer of "Gestalt" is a good example of this creation of gratitude. Sarton offers praise for God's grace and forbearance, for God's discipline, and for both the light and the dark of God's being—that which is known and that which still remains a mystery. This closing meditation once more suggests the joys of solitude while denying that solitude is paradisiacal. Her realistic portrait of solitude helps readers see the best of it while preventing them from romanticizing her or it.

This theme of gratitude in the midst of spiritual austerity continues in "Christmas Letter, 1970," which celebrates the work of Marynia Farnham, a gifted counselor and friend of Sarton's. This poem represents an early example of her Christmas poems—a special gift Sarton would personally send to her fans (and eventually publish) every holiday season from the mid-1970s until her death in 1995. Without proselytizing for a particular faith, these Christmas poems adopt the Christian metaphors of the season and broaden them into ways of conceiving of and thinking about the heart and spirit.

Sarton begins her Christmas meditation by discussing the hunger and desire that seemingly burst from below ground throughout the winter. She uses the metaphors of winter flower bulbs and a stray cat to describe the desire she feels. Winter bulbs, Sarton writes, struggle to live in the cold cellar and come to represent those who are sick. The homeless cat who hungers for food, shelter, and acceptance represents Sarton and her desire to save (the cat, others, and perhaps herself) and be saved.[5] Ultimately Sarton acknowledges that Christmas often exacerbates these drives and desires, making it perhaps the saddest time of the year.

Farnham, through her practice as a psychotherapist, is able to accomplish this healing of desire in others, a talent Sarton considers a magic art, comprised of the ability to care, listen, offer suggestions and answers, and provide a safe haven for those in distress—a talent Sarton hopes to emulate.[6] Sarton also articulates what a therapist should not do: that is, she should not have a set agenda about what recovery should look like and she should neither dispense nor encourage guilt. While the therapist does provide shelter to her patients, they must neither rest there nor fall into love with the therapist, but instead they should dig deeper into their own reality to find answers. Once they achieve these answers they will be lightened of their burdens and can soar away from the safe haven.

Sarton recognizes the same potential in herself to save the lives of others from despair and self-destruction. In fact in her analogy to the Incarnation (the birth of Jesus Christ) Sarton suggests that we can all be inborn with a redemptive spirit and presence. She recognizes that we will die inside many times in our search for redemption but we will eventually find tentative wings on which to fly.

Thus *A Durable Fire* brings the reader on a search for the spirit which resides within all of us and occasionally gets injured or lost. Sarton celebrates finding this source and center in the final poem of the collection, "The Contemplation of Wisdom." Sarton here argues that wisdom steps in as the answer to all sorts of loss and heartache, and indeed she has repeatedly shown this process in this collection's poems by chronicling her battle to move from loss to truth.

Halfway to Silence **(1980)**

What makes *Halfway to Silence* an important volume for Sarton is not only the inclusion of her critically acclaimed poem "Old Lovers at the Ballet" but also what leads to the creation of this poem and other insightful milestones. Aged into her early sixties by the time she composes the poetry in this volume, Sarton traces the landscape of finding new romance in later life, an increasingly important concern in an era of longer lifetimes and later, even multiple, marriages. Sarton's journey in *Halfway to Silence* charts this path of love for those long accustomed to being alone and shows both the highs and lows that accompany love and the myriad of sacrifices that also accompany it.

In sections 1 and 2 of this volume Sarton chronicles these emotional vagaries of love in later life. The narrative begins with the finding of a new and unexpected passion in the poem "After All These Years." Even the title, with the extra emphatic "All," amplifies the nature of the long duration between this and Sarton's last experience of love. Sarton relates that she had grown comfortable alone with her cat and dog, never expecting again to feel the passion of a love affair. She describes the finding of this love as tumultuous, suggesting that passionate intimacy (conveyed in the poem through the repetition of the act of kissing) brings with it both heightened sensation and heightened disruption. Her small nucleus is shaken once more by an earthquake of Eros.

THE SAGE EMERGES

Her next mention of this love affair comes in the poem "A Voice," where Sarton discovers that with new love she finds a new part of herself deep within. She commits fully and honestly to seek this voice out of the depths of her soul and live in the realizations that it will bring. Yet to live in this honesty leads again to vulnerability and pain, as she relates in "The Balcony." For Sarton the reawakening of Eros brings reward along with the pain as she describes a tranquil moment for her and her lover. She recognizes that this love is still new, making it both more intense and more vulnerable. She and her lover have not built up a lifetime of knowledge and commitment, nor are they living over again the past recriminations that make so many long-term relationships sterile. She sees her love as fated and recognizes the potential that something beautiful and lasting can come out of this relationship through its pains and pleasures.

As the relationship grows, Sarton acknowledges the need for the pace of the affair to slow down so that the long, joyous, and languorous process of getting to know one another body and soul can begin. She characterizes this as the "Time for Rich Silence" in a relationship—after the first fires have cooled slightly but there is still so much underneath to know and explore. Again Sarton returns to the imagery of disruption, recognizing and valuing not only the beauty but also the darkness and danger of erotic awakening.

Sarton begins to search for language to describe these days of quiet completeness, finally concluding that love is one of the "Three Things" that, like wind in the trees and water flowing in a brook, cannot ultimately be verbalized. The "First Autumn" of this love brings the first significant chill to the relationship and with it the promise of grief and the affirmation that the lovers are still bonded.

Sadly, however, the ensuing winter brings a bitter end to the promise unrealized in this still-new affair. Sarton loses her lover, who rejects her in "Mal du Départ," and though she must work through the pain of this loss, she recognizes that these departures are part of life.

From these experiences Sarton draws conclusions about the nature of Eros ("The Country of Pain"), insights about the triumphs of old age ("Old Lovers at the Ballet"), and new thoughts about the power of inspiration ("Of The Muse"). In "The Country of Pain" Sarton presents love as leading to pain and describes the land of Eros as a country of pain. This country is a place where each stands alone, only finding communion in the occasional joy that accompanies lovemaking. Further she suggests that those in love are often punished like children, perhaps for their tears and their quest for truth beneath the hard exterior of the rock and soil. The people in this country may once have thought of love as easy but have now come to realize their mistake.

Three mythic figures reside in this land—Medusa, Circe, and Eros. Medusa in "The Country of Pain" more closely resembles the traditional image of the woman whose gaze turns others to stone than the welcome if intimidating image of the dark side of oneself that ultimately promises healing (found in Sarton's earlier poem "The Muse as Medusa"). Medusa facilitates the hardening of love, thus symbolizing the force that transforms love into pain. She is the queen of this realm and as the poem ends she begins anew her complete domination of the realm of love. Circe, described in book 10 of Homer's *Odyssey,* lures men and then transforms them into swine. Sarton alludes to Circe's power over these transformed beings, suggesting that Circe has changed each one personally. The fate of those transformed is shown as terrible.

THE SAGE EMERGES

All of these characters culminate in the personification of Eros, whom this land represents. Sarton describes erotic love as sad and unpredictable. She hopes desperately for someone to save those who have fallen victim to it but she recognizes that they may not be seeking salvation. When Eros is in her happy phase, love is lavish, abundant, and luxurious; when love ends and Eros collapses in depression, Circe and Medusa take over to finish off her victims. Thus the arena of Eros ultimately is synonymous with the country of pain that comes at the end of a love affair.

Sarton's exploration of the land of love, which culminates in "The Country of Pain," becomes the fodder that produces the two most important poems of this collection: "Old Lovers at the Ballet" and "The Muse." "Old Lovers at the Ballet," probably Sarton's most important later poem, begins with an interesting but deceptively predictable comparison between ballerinas on the stage, in the glory of their youth and vitality, and two elderly viewers feeling sadness at their lost vivacity.[7] The dancers symbolize the combination of art and energy, suggesting that perhaps Yeats's desire to separate the dancer and the dance (found at the end of "Among School Children") was misguided. The dancers' every step is flawless and their every move is perfectly planned and disciplined to produce their art. The old lovers, by contrast, are physically inactive, merely viewers instead of dancers. They feel sadness when they compare their bodies to those of the dancers; age, which has altered them, seems to make jest of them.

The last line of the second stanza, however, suggests that appearances can be deceptive. This line and the two stanzas that follow present a different reality, portraying the lovers as the more gifted ones when considered in light of the spiritual wisdom and vitality they possess. The young are still awkward and weak at the level of their souls, whereas the souls of the two lovers are graceful and athletic, not full of burning physical energy but nurtured on the spiritual light of the Holy Spirit. In other words the old lovers are in touch with the source of all life and light through the Holy Spirit, who makes them walk in glorious light.

At heart, though, this poem is not only a beautiful and moving evocation of old age as an ideal time which transcends physical limitations. It also represents Sarton finally wresting herself away from the works of Yeats, one of her foremost poetic models. Catherine B. Emanuel's careful study of this poem and its antecedents offers additional insights into Sarton's craft and ideas. Emanuel maintains that the poem is based on the musical form of the fugue, in which two or more distinct themes conflict and resolve.[8] Emanuel points out that the image of the soul clapping is an allusion to Yeats's "Sailing to Byzantium" and, through that poem, to William Blake (116). According to Emanuel Sarton leaves the gender of the lovers deliberately ambiguous in order to suggest a wide range of relational possibilities and—in imitation of Yeats—builds the structure of the poem around the "contraries" of "youth and age, sickness and health, body and soul" (116–18). Emanuel argues that Sarton's verse is more positive, more feminist, and more spiritual than that of its predecessor: "By 'transforming' Yeats's poem, Sarton provides a subtle but radical change: . . . the journey transcends the physical; Sarton's old lovers merely contemplate the dance, and the moving spectacle of art is enough to move them into a triumphant spiritual realm" (116). Emanuel concludes that the lovers have to step symbolically out of the dark in order to embody the light, taking a leap-of-faith with no guarantees (119). Thus Emanuel argues that Sarton chooses to focus not upon the losses of old age, as Yeats does, but "upon the triumphs" enjoyed as one grows older (127).

The final poem of *Halfway to Silence* explores Sarton's lifetime of experience with poetic inspiration. Sarton recognizes that as she ages she has gained a new perspective on inspiration. In "Of the Muse" Sarton sketches both her former and emergent understanding of this creative source. As critics have noted, Sarton's muses prior to this point were most often women she loved deeply and unrequitedly. In her mid-sixties Sarton's muse becomes less human and embodied, more mystical and spiritual.

In "Of the Muse" Sarton reflects that she has recently gone through a dry period because of her pride, her lies, and her misunderstanding of the nature of the muse. She manages, however, to overcome this dry period when she discovers that poetry can only grow from striving for candidness between herself and her readers. Sarton attempts to conquer the negative elements of the self—its lusts, pride, and vanity—and she seeks out a place of spiritual openness. Sarton argues here that spiritual openness means being fully willing to cast oneself into the void without presupposing what meaning or resolution one may find. By allowing herself to be open and let the muse lead where she will, Sarton discovers a spiritual illumination that brings renewal in its wake and causes even a cold winter day to speak the promise of newness.

Halfway to Silence marks Sarton at her strongest in terms of her commitment to candor and to the places where love and poetry lead. Many people, including Sarton's biographer and perhaps even some of her fans and lovers, have noted Sarton's extremes of emotion and even her petulance. Yet the literary record she leaves is invariably enriched by these same emotions and allows others to admit their own humanness. The affair Sarton chronicles in this volume is far from ideal for her or the other woman, and not all the blame conveniently lies with the other woman. In this collection Sarton acknowledges her own foibles (as in "Of the Muse") and she explores her intense feelings of fear (as in "A Winter Notebook"). These admissions allow the reader to see Sarton as a real person rather than as a construct put on public display. This commitment to honesty at all costs leads her readers to a fuller, more honest look at their own lives and love affairs—even (and especially) those which did not bear the purest fruits.

Letters from Maine (1984)

In *Letters from Maine* Sarton faces old age, finally arriving at some acceptance of the limits and joys of being in her mid-seventies. It is a time for gaining a deeper awareness of the renewing power of the cycles of the body and the earth, and it is also a time of significant losses, as some individual poem titles suggest (such as the poignant elegy "Mourning to Do"). Ultimately it is a time of a deeper, more spiritual understanding of the self and its relationship to loss and growing older.

The title sequence, "Letters from Maine," explores the depths of love during a time of increasing solitude in Sarton's life. Two poems preface this long title sequence and establish the themes and boundaries she is about to explore. With "Contemplation of Poussin" Sarton opens the volume by considering the world of art. Sarton, though, sees that world as bleak and disordered; she feels in the poem that she is in essence devouring her own heart.

Sarton longs for art to bring a refuge for her pain, yet even the apparently quiet world of pastoral retreat she envisions carries its own poison. Sarton wishes for the world of the painter Nicolas Poussin and the composer Wolfgang Amadeus Mozart, but she clothes within that desire an equally strong quest for death. The world of Mozart and Poussin is for Sarton a place "where men and women drink to end their pain."[9] Although she later suggests wine is this drink (alluding perhaps to her own problems with alcohol[10]), the numerous drowned lovers found in pastoral poetry surely color her thoughts here.

Realizing that art and death can indeed be linked, Sarton questions art itself, wondering if it can ever be separated from that which causes injury and pain. In stanza 5 of "Contemplation of Poussin" Sarton raises three questions regarding this perplexity: First, can artistic creation exist without a concomitant and unhealthy addiction to drink? Second, can art emerge without the love of another woman who, with her attention, turns lust into true love? And third, can art survive without any hiding and evasion?

These queries prompt Sarton to seek an art not wed to the destruction of the soul. However—at least here—this quest is unfruitful. She sadly concludes in "Contemplation" that art must grow out of love's pain. Without this pain Sarton has to admit that there are no answers.

Sarton then moves to her next prefatory poem, "A Farewell." In this poem Sarton explores the ways to deal with the endings of romantic relationships. Sarton posits that there are two unhealthy, unproductive responses to the breakup of an affair: The first is to retreat into an idealized image of the past relationship. The second is to enact repression by charging blindly and forcefully ahead, never fully acknowledging the pain and loss or the lessons that could be learned from them.

Rather than these two paths, Sarton recommends a third, more emotionally healthy option: to allow the pain to subside of its own accord. She imagines this process as a type of communion out of which will come wisdom and discernment. Bobby Caudle Rogers reminds us that the rhyme scheme of this poem is "at once staid and unbalanced, as the emotions underlying the events" that Sarton recalls "must have been."[11] Sarton mimics in her prosody the ebb and flow of nature's cycle and the connected cycle of love, loss, and recovery.

From the world of art as imagined in "Contemplation" and the world of pain and recovery described in "A Farewell," Sarton formulates her major poetic sequence "Letters from Maine" as a bridge into a minute documentation of the end of a love affair and the possible wisdom that comes in the guise of art. The initial section of the sequence is set in November, symbolically representing a time of death, decay, silence, and loneliness. Jane Miller describes this silence as "aggressive" and "adversarial," not docile, leading ultimately to "recognition, cognition, and excavation."[12] At least initially Miller's description of the silence as aggressive and perhaps even adversarial is fitting.

Even nature in November, at the end of a cycle of growth and fruitfulness, depresses Sarton. Her carefully constructed environment (which includes her Maine home), her carefully tended garden, and her various routines that fill the days there, offer no consolation for or reconciliation to the absence of her beloved. Sarton addresses her lover and through her, surreptitiously, her reader, asking them to meet her in the silences of the poem, perhaps hoping that together they can reform this silence. She imagines that through the silences she and others may find healing.

In the second poem of the sequence Sarton raises the issue of her age, situating her recent love affair as potentially one of her last. She reluctantly begins to accept that the tenor of old age is not passion and robust love but solitude, which perhaps can ultimately serve to nurture her. She strives to set her feelings outside of time's pale continuance in hopes of savoring and reviewing this short-lived experience.

Using the metaphor of a kite and its guide, Sarton envisions her muse in poem 3 as anchoring and guiding her as she flies aloft. Although both good and bad news inundate Sarton's quiet, domestic world, she remains untouched, able to rise before dawn to greet the new day. In a manner reminiscent of John Donne's poem "A Valediction Forbidding Mourning," Sarton is anchored by her muse, which allows her safely to soar high without losing her bearings.

In his extensive study of this sequence Rogers alludes to its free verse form, suggesting that it does not "numb the reader" as some free verse does, but instead is used by Sarton "as a strategy to heighten the pain. . . . Writing of grief in free verse is an act of courage . . . rather than an attempt at anesthesia."[13] The verse form allows Sarton to chart the ebb and flow of this love affair in poem 4 as she wonders how it can be both within time and outside of it. Lovers, Sarton reflects, are both lost and found, both hopeful and despairing. She thus explicates the paradoxical nature of being in love and of the feelings that accompany it.

The fifth poem of the sequence raises the specter of danger to the relationship. Looking out at the ocean from her Maine home, Sarton sees her emotions and their undercurrents as they threaten to burst through, fatally crashing her and the love affair against the rocks. She hopes her lover is safe somewhere behind the mountains, hidden from the tumult of the sea. Sarton prepares, knowing that her lover is safe, to ride the currents in a detached and reflective way.

In the sixth poem Sarton seeks a primal source that will provide answers to the trouble emerging in the relationship and perhaps redeem the disturbing silences. Sarton envisions this primal source as the old woman in Nootka tribal mythology who brings Sarton artistic renewal and fertility, speaking the words "*strength, laughter, [and] endurance.*"[14] As Rogers identifies, these words correspond respectively to the trees, the ocean, and the woman's heart (images that appear in the poem prior to the old woman's words).[15] Ultimately these words and images reimagine the silences not as places of terror, adversity, and despair, but as places of growth for art and living.

Sarton speculates in poem 7 of the sequence that what may be at the heart of her emotional and artistic problems is a dearth of positive images of the aged or of the process of growing old. She wonders if anyone "has imagined the unicorn grown old."[16] The task of combining the magical and the elderly, not merely of envisioning the old unicorn as a model, becomes for Sarton the key to healing and to creating art out of this loss of love late in her life.[17]

The finality of the relationship crowds out even nature's abundance in poem 8. When her lover ends the affair Sarton's world goes black. She goes through the standard self-recriminations: Did I push too hard? Did I want too much? She also wonders if her desire to turn love into poetry may be the cause of the breakup. She concludes, however, that these questions are practically unanswerable. Sarton is letting go and moving on even though it seems impossible in this moment of despair to imagine how.

Spring arrives both literally and symbolically in poem 9 as the muse clears the inner world of the poet. The metaphor of spring cleaning structures the poem. As the muse enacts the dirty work of preparing the poet's mind for the summer season, the poet herself is left free of guilt to become completely open to the flow of the ocean and the resonances of nature. The muse thus functions almost as hired help. When the muse comes to do her work, the poet is revitalized and the answers to the pressing questions of poem 8 finally come from within the poet herself in the form of reflection.

Poem 10 resonates with this new life and increased possibility. The waters herein are baptismal, suggesting both the burial of an old self and the enactment of a new birth.[18] The poet now lives in a protected area within herself, safe from the spiritual dangers of the world. Sarton lets the muse accomplish her work and she therefore finds peace and consolation. She now can step forth from the tomb of the relationship (and metaphorically the body of the poem itself) to walk again in the light.

Thus the sequence "Letters from Maine" combines spiritual longing with a recovery from physical and emotional displacement, representing in its style the struggle the poet undergoes and overcomes. Sarton responds fully within this sequence to the issues raised in "Contemplation of Poussin" concerning art's illusions; in so doing she creates a poetry of pain and longing that brings real resolution as it depicts real life. She also conquers the pain of "A Farewell" through the act of creating art and helping the reader experience the move from a silence that is aggressive and adversarial to a silence that nurtures and sustains the writer at her spiritual center.

In "Mourning to Do" Sarton returns to the vales of loss and pain and faces one of the most terrible losses of all: the death of her longtime friend and sometime companion Matlack. Sarton's phrasing in the poem suggests that Matlack's struggles with Alzheimer's are over and therefore Matlack is also freed from the darkness. Sarton faces the dark despair of loss and her conception of what those years of decline must have felt like to Matlack, recognizing that she cannot comprehend either the depth of her own pain and loss or of Matlack's pain during the decline.[19]

Sarton is able, through the writing process, to accept Matlack's loss with a combination of intense grief and immense relief that the suffering is over. Memories of the good times, as well as a full reckoning with the pain of the bad, come to nourish Sarton through her grief and she concedes that Matlack's life had hardly been worth sustaining during her last days. Thus Sarton recognizes but does not reconcile the pain and ambiguity of loss when one has suffered terribly from disease before dying.

The volume *Letters from Maine* truly represents the manner in which Sarton labels the time of growing old—a "Magnificat of severe joys."[20] Referring here to the Virgin Mary's song of praise that celebrates the news of the impending conception and birth of the Christ child (found in the gospel of St. Luke[21]), Sarton once more reaches back to the feminine and to feminist sources for her art, recognizing that women's art is often raw, painful, and distorting of the standard genres. Unable to write pastoral poetry and unable to mask her feelings, Sarton seeks an art that recreates her pain at the same time as it brings renewal and wholeness. The volume *Letters from Maine* in essence becomes a praise or "Magnificat" of the blessedly feminine values of nurture and forbearance, as well as a recognition that from severe, heart-rending pain, "severe joys" can come in the end.

The Silence Now (1988)

In her title poem for this volume Sarton poses a series of questions about the nature of silence in old age. Sarton recognizes that the later years bring with them a minimizing of want simply because a person can no longer obtain and achieve the things she used to. The answer to these questions for Sarton is to become much more mystical and altruistic: what she wants is for the world to begin to adopt a fundamental ethic—based on compassion and mutual recognition of the humanity in each of us—that celebrates each other's individuality and talents.

The Silence Now develops this ethic through lyric poetry and suggests that true compassion could offer revolutionary change and growth for America. Although progress and change are by nature slow, Sarton's survey of her life and times shows that some progress has occurred. As Sarton explores aging in her own life, she finds in her mother and other friends models for this kind of love, strength, and lifelong commitment to improving oneself and others. She uses these lives as examples for how to negotiate the overwhelming silences of old age and of life in general in the later twentieth century.

Due to illness, including a mild stroke and the first signs of breast cancer, and the loss of friends and mobility, Sarton's own state, as described in the opening of this volume, is close to despairing. She resents the many demands that people, especially fans, still put on her to produce and be wise. She states in the poem "Salt Lick" that she may soon be used up completely. Sarton wonders at this late point in her life where renewal can come from—or if it can come at all. How to age well and remain giving, vibrant, and growing for herself and others becomes Sarton's focus in the poetry of this volume.

Sarton's answer for how to fulfill this quest comes initially from studying others who seemed to age well and remain compassionate and giving late into their lives. The first such model she considers is her mother, who died in the late 1940s. Sarton reflects in the poem "Dream" on her own lingering grief over her mother's death, suggesting at first that she still feels the only way to recover from this loss is to die herself. However Sarton soon begins to reconsider this initial, emotional response and she begins to hope that her mother's life and death can be a source of strength. Sarton thus seeks to acknowledge and grow from one of the most painful losses in her life.

After the resolution of "Dream" Sarton begins to celebrate her mother's glowing legacy of gardening and love in "August Third," titled in reference to her mother's birthday. Sarton reflects that despite her mother having often been ill and exhausted, she was nonetheless able to endure and find the strength to plant flowers and serve a friend in need. This strength of Mabel Sarton's challenges Sarton to overcome her own lethargy and sadness in the face of aging and death, and thus becomes both an encouragement to her and a source of guilt: since her mother was able to triumph over illness, Sarton reflects that she should be able to also.

Sarton hopes that her mother's spirit will still walk with her and help her achieve her mother's inner strength and drive. The test for Sarton is not merely surviving but continuing to live and grow even into the years of illness and loss. Sarton finds in her mother both an abiding presence and a challenging example.

For additional lessons on growing old and still giving Sarton looks to friends who are older than she and still surviving and growing. In her poem "Two Birthdays" Sarton celebrates the lives of Keith Warren and Edith Morse Johnson. Warren has just celebrated his eightieth birthday and Sarton reflects on the lessons she still learns from him. He represents for her someone who is deeply centered, growing both tall and deep. Because of his depth he is able to maintain balance and evidence the virtues of love and courage. His presence is peaceful and Sarton concludes that he teaches her how to accept change and lack of capacity.

Where Warren provides a model of stability, deep growth, and peacefulness, Johnson offers an example of someone who is still alive and feisty even into her ninetieth year.[22] Johnson successfully resists weariness and despair—two emotions Sarton herself struggles against constantly in her seventies—and provides a model of how to will oneself out of loneliness. Johnson is a teacher still visited and celebrated by her students' grandchildren, a remarkable legacy of a life well lived. She is characterized as still being actively engaged in life. Sarton concludes with a tone of encouragement and a sense of awe at Johnson's example.

Sarton's study of grace-filled aging leads her ultimately to consider old age at its best as "A House of Gathering," where there is more to do than ever. If lived correctly, this time of old age can become a period of deepening and adjustment. The vital lesson, Sarton realizes, is valuing what can yet be done and seeing even that little bit in all its magnitude and worth. While she may not be able to overthrow tyrants, perhaps the simple act of nurturing and growing is revolutionary and can ultimately save our society. From all of these examples Sarton therefore suggests that the best we can do is continue to "work, love, [and] be silent" and from this silence learn to "speak."[23]

Sarton envisions this centered, balanced, enriching act of speech as emerging from a life of reflection and compassionate action. The first place where real change can occur is in the nurturing of and caring for those who are ill. As she did in her earlier poem

"Night Watch," Sarton argues in "To Those in the Limbs of Illness" that we need to love those who are ill and perhaps dying. Love, she maintains, will help them to overcome their illness, to transcend it and perhaps even spiritually grow from it.

No illness stood more fully in need of understanding and care in the late 1980s than AIDS. Sarton addresses AIDS in a poem of that title, hoping her readers can overcome their fears and reach forth in love to make a difference. The care and concern for those who are victims of AIDS becomes in Sarton's world another place where we can enact love.

As Sarton views the 1980s from this perspective, she sees both progress and room remaining for growth. She writes approvingly in her "New Year Poem" of people who have begun to garden and fathers who have stepped out of the traditional masculine role to assume nurturing characteristics. Like Adrienne Rich in her poem "Atlas of a Difficult World," Sarton recognizes that these shifts in gender roles and these more holistic approaches to life and earth represent real promise. She asks her readers not to stop with these examples of progress but to move on to the real change and growth forecasted. Sarton ultimately inverts one of the beatitudes from the Sermon on the Mount (recorded in the gospel of St. Matthew[24]), suggesting that we must achieve our inheritance of the earth and save it through renewed meekness. She envisions not the scriptural form of a passive meekness that will be rewarded by God giving the earth to those who practice it, but rather an active claiming of the earth by those who can save it. Thus Sarton's ethic of compassion and care can be realized.

The silence alluded to in the title of this collection is one that ultimately leads to compassionate speech and action. Sarton hopes through these examples that her readers can learn to live this life of ethic that is based on care and concern. Sarton argues that our standard modes of life and speech ultimately could lead, both figuratively and literally, to a loss of the earth and a death of the great possibilities yet to be realized in so many aspects of our democracy. By learning to be silent and learning to act compassionately in listening and action, Sarton suggests that we can create a small revolution that will lead to real change and hope.[25]

Coming into Eighty **(1994)**

> I write poems, have always written them, to transcend
> the painfully personal and reach the universal.[26]

Sarton's last volume is a pared-down meditation on old age and American society during and immediately following the Gulf War of 1991. The finale of her career as a poet, these poems represent Sarton practicing her ideal of pure lyric—brief, luminous images and statements that fuse into an effective aesthetic whole. None of the poems of this collection are lengthy. Like the life of the elderly itself, these are small, perfect moments salvaged from the weaknesses and illnesses that ravage the aged.

Sarton writes in her preface about the unique situation she was in when these poems came to her. An aging writer, Sarton reflects that she has learned to "live with essences, with what is innermost . . . because what is outermost is often beyond my strength."[27] These essences suggest Sarton's arrival at essential and universal truths detailed in almost crystalline images. As a writer in solitude during her latter years, Sarton recognizes that she now has "more time for being and less ability to do then ever before," so that even the act of poetry making can only be achieved in odd and translucent moments of health.[28]

The writing of these poems comes about because of the demands of a kitten named Pierrot which entered Sarton's life through Heilbrun, Sarton's friend and literary executor. After her cat Tamas's death, Sarton had divulged that if she ever had a cat again she would prefer a Himalayan. Heilbrun found just the kitten for her—a white "hurricane" named Pierrot.[29] Pierrot consistently awakened Sarton at three and four in the morning to let him out. During these times Sarton found herself inspired and began jotting down lines, images, and notes that would become the poems of *Coming into Eighty*. Thus this final volume of poems is dedicated to the cat Pierrot. This tremendous final outpouring of verse ended when a friend graciously, but perhaps unfortunately, established a cat door in Sarton's basement so Pierrot could get in and out as he pleased.

Sarton recognizes the different quality of these poems from that which she had written before, both in terms of inspiration and content. "These poems [are] . . . a new kind of poem for me," Sarton writes. "They came of their own free will and I had only to accept radical change and use it as best I could."[30] The "radical change" Sarton here notes is both at the level of what inspires the poems and how she composes them. Before this volume most of Sarton's poetry was inspired by the love of another person and composed during her morning writing sessions at her desk. Sarton's discipline and her ritual of establishing a particular set of hours in which to write every day make her a highly successful and motivating example to others, and indicate just how demanding and irritated she could be whenever her time scheme was broken unexpectedly. As her biographer Peters notes, most of Sarton's poems were inspired by love affairs and friendships with others, mainly women. When the poems of *Coming into Eighty* are written, Sarton is neither in love nor working within her normal disciplined routine. Rather these come unexpectedly and must either be lost or adopted through her willingly altering her lifestyle.

In this volume Sarton offers a final, profound look at the experiences and pain of aging. Three themes come to the fore in this regard, which, while apparent in other late works, all reach prominence and culmination in this volume. The first of these themes concerns Sarton learning to accept dependency and enfeeblement. Tasks such as getting dressed become dangerous as she realizes that an accidental fall could cost her dearly, and they thus lead to both celebration and exhaustion when successfully completed. The second of the three themes reveals Sarton recounting the accumulated loss of family and friends throughout a long and productive life. She celebrates those who have been gone for years but are still mourned, such as her mother ("For My Mother") and poet, teacher, and muse Jean Dominique, who taught Sarton how to age gracefully and whom Sarton wishes she could hear again ("To Have What I Have"). Sarton also sadly notes those who are dying now, such as school friends from her early days ("Best Friend"); those from her initial days as a writer in England associated with the Bloomsbury group ("Obit"); and those creative souls who are dying and dead prematurely because of AIDS ("After the Long Enduring" and "Elegy," both of which are dedicated to Charles Barber).

The third theme evident in this volume is Sarton facing her own impending death. Like many who are seriously ill, Sarton must face the ambivalence of wanting to die (as noted in stanza 1 of "Wanting to Die") and yet not wanting to let go of the good things quite yet (as noted in stanza 2 of the poem). This journey into death and the hereafter occupies Sarton's mind as she considers what leaving her body behind could mean. Will death bring annihilation or entry into new and unimagined realms of the spirit? While recognizing that no one knows for sure, Sarton embraces a kind of metaphysical hope, turning once more to nature in "The O's of November" and wondering if the patterns of death and rebirth that she sees there are also experienced by the human soul.

Sarton meditates on the fact that these poems are inspired by and contain images from the domestic realm. She chronicles and invests the domestic with deep and universal significance. In one poem, for instance, Sarton uses the act of rinsing her eye with medicine as a metaphor for sanctification (the act of spiritual cleansing). In this poem, "Rinsing the Eye," she describes old age and infirmity as a barrier that separates her from experiencing the world more fully. The eye when rinsed, however, clears the soul for an act of memory that is sacramental. Sarton writes that her vision then focuses on a garden within her, which is probably a description of her own Maine garden but also represents the soul that is still growing even through loss. She states that memory itself is what saves her and clears her eye, making memory a savior for Sarton as she faces life in her eighties.

The apparent simplicity of a daily chronicling of old age and a focus on domestic imagery hides how close the political and social are to Sarton's art. Sarton has lost none of the social commentary that is a profound element of her earlier works, such as her poetry collection *A Grain of Mustard Seed.* Rather it is transformed; for what Adrienne Rich states about the bedroom is also generally true of the domestic in Sarton's verse: "[It] is never far removed from what happens in the streets."[31]

In "The Use of Force" Sarton uses the act of taking Pierrot to the veterinarian as a metaphor for the United States's use of force in the Gulf War of 1991. Earlier in the volume, in the poem "Small Joys," the reader sees Pierrot in his full cat glory. Now, in "The Use of Force," Pierrot and Sarton are both victims of the use of force to get him into his cat carrier for the trip to the vet. Sarton writes that Pierrot's dignity and self-esteem are damaged by his being forcibly confined. She observes, though, that both "victim" and "perpetrator" are hurt by acts of force, for the perpetrator comes to feel guilt and pain. Sarton too was bruised by this act and her response is one of remorse and tears for herself, Pierrot, and other victims and abusers.

Thus "The Use of Force" breaks down the apparent dichotomy between victims and abusers. Sarton calls for compassion and understanding for both sides of this sad equation. In the context of this volume Sarton also clearly sees the United States involved in an unnecessary and misguided use of force against Iraq, an enemy she claims is already much weaker than America.

The aphoristic poem "A Thought" captures the principle that underlies Sarton's Gulf War poems. She writes that when a steam-roller crushes a butterfly it accomplishes nothing but the destruction of worth and beauty. She argues that the beautiful, which includes flowers, butterflies, children, and a life of peace, is worth much more than mere conquest. But following her analysis through suggests that beauty is in essence quite fragile and easily lost, hurt, and destroyed.

In her journal *Endgame* Sarton chronicles her day-to-day reactions to the events leading up to the Gulf War; in *Encore* she chronicles her reactions to its outcome. She builds these disparate and daily feelings into the principles of nonviolence described in the Gulf War poems "The Absence of God" and "All Souls 1991." In "The Absence of God" Sarton suggests that if one looks around at the world it appears as if God is dying or disappearing. Sarton feels impotent in the face of so much catastrophe and calamity. She suggests that our ability to care has been short-circuited because we do not believe we can make a difference. Sarton therefore calls out to her reader to do something, anything to make a difference so others can once more see God—and her call is urgent.

Sarton continues here the criticism of President George Bush's administration that she had begun in her journals. Many moderates and liberals felt that the Gulf War was unnecessary and was primarily a political move to detract focus from increasing domestic problems that Bush seemed ill-prepared for and uninterested in solving. Sarton's lyrical call for compassionate action thus works at all levels: from the homebound invalid who can remain informed, pray, and give what she can, to national leaders who choose to wage war and create enemies rather than face their society and its problems head-on.

Sarton continues this critique in "All Souls 1991," focusing more emphatically on the children of Iraq who are victimized by the United States's intervention in the Persian Gulf. The Iraqi children are so traumatized, Sarton notes, that they live in a perpetual state of shock, unable even to express their grief. In a rhymed couplet at the end of the poem Sarton asks the reader to consider the cost of the war in more than terms of victory or defeat. The concluding irony of this couplet suggests that indeed we could ask for more than just victory: for more care, for more love, for less unnecessary suffering placed on others for the sake of politics, profit, and patriotism. In her journal *Encore* (in an entry dated 9 August 1991) Sarton quotes an article written by John Pilger (printed in *The New Statesman)* that points out the overwhelming cost of this apparently unnecessary war: Pilger records that 170,000 Iraqi children were expected to die in the coming year as a result of the war; that up to 250,000 had died because of the war; that 1.8 million Iraqis were then homeless; and that the infrastructure of the country was destroyed, paving the way for famine and epidemic. The most ironic part of all, Pilger claims, is that Saddam Hussein was prepared to withdraw from Kuwait even without the war.

Sarton concludes, "It is so terrible to think that Bush is a national hero and that somehow or other nobody in America thinks about this or takes responsibility for it. So it is a huge festering cancer of irresponsibility and stark sadism at the center of our civilization—if it can now be called that."[32] The poems reflect Sarton's belief that the United States had not risen to the challenge of keeping its own domestic sphere in order and had channeled much of that disorder into a useless war that cost another nation far too much.

Coming into Eighty thus presents complex glimpses into the life of the aged and the life of the country in the early 1990s. As a document of its times it raises profound questions about the nature of the Gulf War and the Bush years, but it also goes well beyond these themes to greater universal issues. By bringing the lyric and lyrical consciousness to bear on her world, Sarton suggests that the domestic can be used to critique the national. Domestic, traditionally feminine ideals and virtues lived out in the household—the virtues of care, compassion, and concern for others, the earth, and the country—can be effective guides to actions on the national and international fronts. The lyric, as realized in Sarton's final poetry, thus becomes an effective if subtle political tool, calling for care and compassion—the household ethic—to find realization in the state. As Sarton clearly claims, change starts with us and our acts of caring for one another.

CHAPTER FOUR

From Europe to America
Early Novels

Sarton's most voluminous output was her nineteen novels. While there are standout volumes of her poetry, Sarton's novels do not maintain the quality or high artistry that her poetry has, nor do they revolutionize the daily lives of her readers in the ways that her journals and memoirs do. One major fault of Sarton's novels is that many are set in a rarefied world—one that is caught between Europe and America, not quite fitting neatly into either category. Of her early novels, only *Faithful Are the Wounds* (1955) and *The Small Room* (1961) manage to successfully bridge that gap. Furthermore Sarton's sense of class status as a member of an academic family, rather upper class in tastes and attitudes, comes through at its worst in many of the novels.

Sarton's first novel, *The Single Hound* (1938), is set in England and Belgium. It centers on the encounter of a young poet named Mark Taylor with an older poet, Dorotheé (nicknamed Doro) Latour, who publishes under the male pseudonym Jean Lateur. As the story begins Doro's publishing career is long over and she now lives as a teacher with three other women known as the "Little Owls." Doro's character is modeled on Jean Dominique, a teacher of Sarton's who also published poetry.[1] Doro hands the poetic torch to Mark and is there to comfort and guide him at the end of his affair with Georgia Manning. The novel offers some insights into art and also aging but they are not completely integrated into the story itself. The writing style of *The Single Hound* is much indebted to Virginia Woolf.

Her second novel, *The Bridge of Years* (1946), catalogs the catastrophes that befell Belgium during World Wars I and II. The shifting fortunes of Belgium are seen through the Duchesne family as they raise their children and twice flee Belgium. Paul, the husband, is a discontented philosopher; Mélanie, the wife, is a designer and interior decorator. There is clearly much semiautobiographical material in this novel since Sarton and her family fled Belgium during World War I and Sarton always looked nostalgically back to Europe. There are clear parallels too between Sarton's parents and the Duchesnes: Sarton's father, George, worked in the academy like Paul (but on the history of science); and Mabel, Sarton's mother, was a designer like Mélanie.

The center of the novel, through whom much of the story is viewed, is Mélanie. Sarton records elsewhere that Mélanie was based in part on Céline Limbosch, a relative of Sarton's whom Sarton depicts most thoroughly in a chapter of her memoir *A World of Light* (1976). Sarton recognized in later years that she had not recognized the negative side of Céline, which included her traits of being rather strongly driven and having a tense and demanding relationship with her daughters. Thus Mélanie comes across in the novel as somewhat ideal and not as fully rounded a character as some of Sarton's other protagonists. The plot centers in many ways around Sarton's remaining nostalgia for the now lost world of Europe that existed before the wars. One of her longest fictional works, though still very much an apprentice novel, it is comprehensive in its depiction of Belgium and what happened to the Belgian people as a result of World Wars I and II.

Sarton's next novel, *The Shadow of a Man* (1950), begins to reflect critically and creatively on Sarton's nostalgia for Europe.

This novel bridges the gap between Europe and America in the character of Francis Albert Chambrier, who in order to become more than the shadow of a man that the title indicates must bridge the gap between his mixed heritage as a son of a French mother and an American father. Francis's bridging reflects Sarton's own as she considers and fictionalizes her own turn toward America. Francis travels to France after his mother's death and, in an attempt to understand his mother's essence and his own identity, comes to know and have an affair with his mother's friend Solánge Bernard. Although he eventually turns his back on Solánge, he is changed from a shadow into a full human and is then able to return and make a family with a woman he has loved but has been unable to commit to. Thus Sarton continues her emphasis on the nuclear family, seeing it at its best after a period of soul-searching for a true self-knowledge that makes the commitment deeper and more honest.

A Shower of Summer Days (1952) traces out a summer when Violet and Charles Gordon, a long-married couple, accept their troubled niece into the quiet world of their home. The Gordons live in England and Sally (the niece) is an American teen in trouble. Sally's mother has sent her to England to get her away from a boyfriend of whom she disapproves. Sally's presence causes the Gordons to open up to their feelings and emotions, including inappropriate sexual attractions, that have lain dormant and repressed behind a facade of civility. Sarton's mastery in this novel is shown in the candid exploration of her characters' deep feelings. Until this point Sarton had not as candidly or fully realized the interior life of her characters, including those emotions that make them and the readers slightly uncomfortable.

The Birth of a Grandfather (1957) explores the few months of coping that a family experiences after the announcement of a pregnancy. The story focuses on Sprig Wyeth, who must mature in order to accept the responsibilities of being a grandfather and of growing older. Sarton will return more successfully to this type of character in the figure of Cornelius Chapman in *Kinds of Love* (1970).

Before turning to the two major novels of her early period, mention must be made of two shorter novellas: *The Fur Person* (1957) and *Joanna and Ulysses* (1963). Her nostalgic tale *The Fur Person* celebrates her cat Tom Jones, a companion for her and Matlack who spent his later life with the author Vladimir Nabokov and his wife. Here Sarton writes what essentially constitutes a fable, imagining the cat's life as a stray and his process of maturing into the perfect "fur person." This work compares interestingly to other reflections on the feline species and its particulars, such as William Burroughs's *The Cat Within.* As Sarton's celebration explores the maturing process in which a cat ideally engages as it grows older, she creates a fable for the move into sensitivity that she sees as the hallmark of maturity in all.

Joanna and Ulysses is a brief fictional chronicle derived from her trip to Greece. Like *The Fur Person* this novella explores the themes of maturity and healing. In it the character Joanna, while visiting the Greek isles, comes to deal with her past as she befriends a donkey named Ulysses. Sarton will later explore this same theme to more effect in *The Poet and the Donkey* (1969).

Sarton's first of two academic novels, *Faithful are the Wounds,* considers the life and death of Edward Cavan, a Harvard professor of American literature and a political liberal.[2] Sarton taps into the changes in America between the 1930s, when a host of liberal programs were established and ideas as radical as communism were freely discussed as possibilities for America, to the 1950s, when such liberalism experienced a backlash under the crusade of Senator Joseph McCarthy and House members of the Un-American Activities Committee, who sought the prosecution of supposed communists. Edward is caught in this change, faced with a country moving into deeper conservatism and colleagues who no longer care to put themselves on the line for their liberal beliefs.

Sarton recognizes in this novel that true liberalism is a sympathetic and caring involvement with and concern for others. Edward envisions it as the coming together of the saints, thus connecting his vision with Christianity. In the conclusion of the novel Edward's friend Damon Phillips makes meaning of Edward's life by standing up proudly and defiantly before Congress. For Sarton the calls of liberalism and defiance are the calls of free speech and connectedness. For, as the novel shows, if injustice happens to one—if one professor is fired over his free speech—and nothing is done, it can and will happen to others.

Sarton's eighth novel, *The Small Room*, is also set in the world of academia. *The Small Room* centers on Appleton, a small but prestigious women's college, and the scandal over a case of plagiarism by one of their best and brightest, a student named Jane Seaman who is a protégée of their most important professor, Carryl Cope. Carryl is involved in a long-term relationship with Olive Hunt, which will be sorely tested and destroyed by this case of plagiarism. Younger faculty and their spouses like Jack and Maria Beveridge survive unscathed and stronger. Sarton frames the controversy as a battle that divides older and younger faculty and threatens two love relationships.

The story is told from the point of view of Lucy Winter, a new professor who has arrived at Appleton after a long-term but failed relationship. Lucy provides an ingenue's position from which to observe the action of the plot. Sarton carefully frames her questions concerning the demands of excellence and the abilities of genius by providing a foil plagiarism case similar to Jane's. Through the detailed explication of the policies and procedures surrounding the plagiarism case of mathematics wizard Olive, the reader learns that there have been other plagiarism cases at Appleton that have led, as the penalty dictates, to expulsion. The final call for Jane's expulsion comes from the student government, a rather odd configuration for most colleges.

Several of Sarton's pervasive themes coalesce in this text, one of her richest novels. The disintegration of Olive and Carryl's relationship results from repressed anger and both women's inability to change even when each knows she is in the wrong. Conversely Maria and Jack's relationship survives because their explosion of anger leads to deeper honesty and openness.

Sarton's advocacy here—revolutionary at the time—for the use of professional counselors on campus ties in with her own commitment to become more candid, honest, and open with herself, and to model that openness for others. Having taught for many years (through the 1960s) at a number of universities, including Harvard, Sarton knew the limits of her ability to deal with students' emotional problems and recognized that in the midst of a push for excellence from the university and professors some students require the support of counselors to help them overcome their emotional hurdles.

Through the characters of female students Olive and Jane, and faculty Carryl and Lucy, Sarton explores the nature of academic excellence for women. The female faculty of Appleton are normally not married or involved in lesbian affairs; they are in pursuit of their lives apart from men. Carryl, as seen through Lucy's eyes, comes to appear venerable but cold. As Lucy grows closer to Carryl, though, she realizes the sacrifices the older woman has made over the years to pursue her excellence. Lucy also begins to realize that successfully providing the education students need means maintaining a level of commitment and devotion beyond that which she had previously thought, a conception that viewed teaching as a mere pastime which could fill up her time until marriage. By the end of the novel Lucy embraces the academic life with all its joys and problems because she still sees the fire in Carryl's eyes and the drive and desire in her for excellence.[3]

CHAPTER FIVE

Philosophical Reflections at Midlife
Mrs. Stevens Hears the Mermaids Singing

Sarton's most critically significant novel is *Mrs. Stevens the Mermaids Singing* (1965). This candid work is Sarton's first to clearly identify her as lesbian in that the protagonist, Hilary Stevens, is also an aging, solitary lesbian author. The book blends autobiography thinly disguised as novel with Sarton's continuing reflections on art, love, and the necessity of solitude. The structure of the novel is a day and the following morning in the life of Hilary. This day is particularly significant because of a major interview occurring in the afternoon, which takes up the bulk of the text. The initial publication of this novel, which in a way marked Sarton's public coming out of the closet, resulted in great personal and professional difficulty for her. Though the book was not well received on its publication in 1965, it was republished in 1973 with a laudatory foreword by Carolyn Heilbrun, at which time it met with much greater success. Thanks in large part to this republication and the promotional efforts of Heilbrun, the work is now considered a classic, early feminist text.

The novel begins with an encounter between the aging protagonist and her young protégé, Mar Hemmer, who is seeking comfort and direction. Mar is trying to come to terms with his homosexuality and seems to be involved in one disastrous affair after another. Hilary's emotions in regard to Mar move from acceptance and love to disgust and rejection, and back again. Part of the reason for this plethora of emotional states is Sarton's own contention in her letters and elsewhere that men who love men and women who love women are radically dissimilar despite the fact that most would link them politically and socially.

In a particularly significant letter, dated 8 March 1954 and addressed to poet Louise Bogan, Sarton expounds on her view of these differences. Sarton had desired a love relationship with Bogan for a number of years but Bogan found Sarton too intense and demanding.[1] In this letter Sarton tries to explain to Bogan what a relationship between women is like. Sarton begins by explaining that she does not believe in the stereotype that one of the women in a lesbian relationship must serve as the male (i.e., be aggressive) and the other one serve as the female (i.e., be submissive). Rather Sarton suggests that a lesbian relationship is like looking in the mirror at oneself, at a double of the same person.[2]

Sarton continues by reflecting on what she sees as the substantive difference between men's and women's approaches to relationships. She argues that women cannot separate sex and love whereas men can. According to Sarton's logic, then, all male homosexuality accordingly "tends toward prostitution," even in good and decent men like W. H. Auden (345). Women, on the other hand, are primarily based in the emotional realm and construct their relationships first and foremost as emotional connections. In an observation that would later have significance for her characterization of Mar, Sarton reflects that "there is nothing wrong for a man in picking up a sailor, but a woman who would do the equivalent would be violating herself" (345).

Sarton concludes this portion of the letter by asserting that the mutual love relationship between two women is thus more powerful than that between two men because men's first drive and "obsession" is always sexual whereas women's is always relational and emotional. "The chances of a complete and happy mutual response are very much greater with two women," Sarton writes, although she then adds the caveat that she has never initiated a woman into a lesbian affair because it could shift the woman dangerously "out of her center" (345).

Thus Sarton sets up in her letter—ten years before she writes the novel—an explanation of the tensions that exist between Hilary and Mar due to Hilary's perspective on male homosexuality. Sarton also forecasts the disastrous results Hilary will experience when she tries to initiate a woman who is not lesbian into a lesbian relationship with her.

When Hilary encounters Mar at the beginning of the day that *Mrs. Stevens Hears the Mermaids Singing* recounts, she is irritated by him and his interruption of her routine.[3] Mar clearly wants to have a sympathetic ear from Hilary but it takes him forever to get to the topic he wants to discuss. Mar's suddenly terminated relationship with a young instructor at Amherst College becomes the subject of their discussion. Mar recounts that he had found himself greatly attracted to Rufus Gilbert. After several meetings in private, Mar and Rufus had become victims of homophobic harassment from the students who are living in the dormitory with Mar. Rufus had sought advice from one of the deans of the college, who then brought Mar in for a discussion which has now made Mar feel horrible and sinful (28). Shortly after this meeting, Rufus and Mar had snuck off campus for their first sexual encounter, which ended with Rufus becoming scared and rejecting Mar, leaving Mar incredibly hurt.

Hilary's reactions during Mar's narrative include her recognition of the differences between Mar's sexuality and her own. She characterizes him as "a wild animal" and seems at times unable to follow the turns of his conversation (23). Later she mentions that she and Mar occasionally get angry with one another (33). Hilary, however, moves beyond Sarton's conception (outlined in the letter to Bogan) of the male homosexual as primarily driven by sex to recognize in Mar the same kinds of feelings she has experienced. She characterizes both of them as people of "primary intensity" who spend their lives in pain but in the end "amount" to something (26). As Mar tries to understand Rufus's reaction and his own pain, Sarton returns to the mirror image she described in her letter to Bogan as the ideal same-sex relationship. Hilary suggests to Mar that he does not understand Rufus yet, does not see things through his eyes. In order to recover Mar must learn to see Rufus through himself, as a type of mirror image. Hilary suggests that the best way she knows for reaching this understanding is to write poetry, an answer that may seem shallow to some but is actually packed with depth and meaning in the novel (31). Although Mar later disappoints Hilary by having a reckless affair with a sailor, thus confirming Sarton's hypothesis about male homosexuality (as delineated in the letter to Bogan), Hilary offers wisdom and recovery for him even in the midst of an occasional inability to understand (205).

Both Hilary's and Sarton's poetry is characterized by coping with pain in relationships. In the novel Hilary explores the emotions behind several volumes of her poetry. What is more significant, however, are Hilary's insights into poetry and the process of poetry making. Hilary's first book of poems came after her husband Adrian's sudden death and her subsequent commitment to a hospital for a year of silence and lack of stimulation because it was believed that she had undergone a nervous breakdown. Hilary states that every book of poems represents a personal breakthrough or "epiphany" (113). Dr. Hallowell, an incredibly creative physician, encourages Hilary to write poetry not about people but objects, which causes Hilary to start looking deep within herself as well as intently at any given object (122). Thus Hilary moves even before her first published book of poems from an abstract poetry of sentimentality to a poetry that harnesses raw emotion in carefully crafted images.

As Hilary works on her poetry she realizes that in order to recapture the intensity she had experienced during the writing exercises that were part of her recovery, she needs an incarnate muse in the form of another person; for Hilary (and Sarton) that muse is primarily female. Interestingly, though, Hilary suggests that Mar and the emotions he has brought into her life are what have inspired her to create the new volume of poetry she has just published before the interview (216). Thus Sarton forecasts her own change of muses for her later poetry—a change away from women and toward other sentient beings (like her cat, for instance, the muse of *Coming into Eighty*).

Hilary laments that the muse for her must always be human (148). She recognizes that the muse brings with her a level of deep and penetrating emotion that then becomes a matter of self-mastery in the poetry itself (151, 154). Because of this close relationship between the human muse and the poet, Hilary states that all her poems are essentially about love, though she uses the term in a very broad sense. According to Hilary, love is both the cause of the poetry and that which is expressed through it (125).

PHILOSOPHICAL REFLECTIONS AT MIDLIFE

Hilary, like Sarton, values the intensity of experience that creates her poetry. At a key moment in the interview which encompasses the majority of the novel, Hilary suggests that this intensity brings with it the form of the poetry it creates, and she points to George Herbert and Thomas Traherne as two poets who also exemplify this relationship between intensity of experience and form of expression (152). Thus Hilary reminds the reader of her own (and by extrapolation, Sarton's) relationship to the metaphysical tradition of poetry from the seventeenth century.

Sarton suggests through Hilary the idea that poetry must arise from the most honest self-expression one can achieve, what Sarton defines via Yeats as "going naked." Sarton writes that this is the true power of the poet; to have any other kind of power inhibits the poet and may even corrupt her art. Sarton maintains in this novel, and later in *The Education of Harriet Hatfield* (1989), that a power that urges an artist to be candid is good while a power that results in sociopolitical clout and material wealth can do nothing but corrupt an artist and cause her to lose her primary focus and intensity (179).

These observations represent the highlights of this candid, philosophical interview that is the centerpiece of *Mrs. Stevens Hears the Mermaids Singing.* Hilary also goes into great depth on other issues relevant to Sarton's life and writing, such as the joys and dangers of solitude, reflections on women writers of the past, and attributes of the female muse. While it is a misnomer to completely equate Hilary with Sarton, the two are parallel poets in many of their theories and practices.

Hilary's past also comes to bear on this interview. *Mrs. Stevens Hears the Mermaids Singing* is often read as a groundbreaking, lesbian, coming-out text, and certainly Sarton and her readers saw it initially in this way. However to view the text solely as a precursor lesbian novel—though this would be appropriate given the life story of Mrs. Stevens—would be to miss the novel's rich philosophical reflections on art.

In all fairness a more apt term for Sarton and Hilary than lesbian would be bisexual, since both had affairs with women and men. Sarton, for instance, had an affair with Julian Huxley before going on to fall in love with his wife, Juliette. In *Mrs. Stevens Hears the Mermaids Singing,* Hilary is married to Adrian Stevens, a dynamic and impulsive man who dies young. Hilary recognizes, as does Adrian's mother, that loving Adrian will consume her life and take her away from her writing if she is not careful. In her discussions with Adrian's mother, Hilary acknowledges that women are often divided when they enter into marriage, caught between the realization of their dreams and desires and the standard sublimation of those to the men they love (39–49). Although Sarton will eventually celebrate some changes in the inequality of the nuclear family—such as men participating in domestic jobs and the rearing of children—she will still note that women are disenfranchised by this institution.

When Adrian dies in a freak riding accident, Hilary falls into the depression that leads to her institutionalization under Dr. Hallowel. After this time, however, Hilary recognizes that her most fervent loves and attractions have been for other women. These lesbian tendencies had surfaced before, most notably in her sexual awakening at age fifteen and the crush she had on her teacher and mentor, Phillipa Munn, who became her first muse (97–108). However, Hilary's most tumultuous affair comes when she meets Willa MacPherson, an affair that leads to disaster because she breaks the dicta Sarton sets forth in her letter to Bogan that one should never initiate a woman into lesbianism who is not already prepared and aware that she needs to explore that side of herself.

Hilary meets Willa at a party for young writers. Hilary is immediately attracted to this talented, older woman and lets Willa know it by bringing her gifts like Johann Sebastian Bach's *Brandenburg Concerti*. When they enter into a conversation about a writer who turns out to be a former lover of Willa's, Hilary empathizes and resonates with Willa's pain. At a slightly later date Hilary discovers Willa alone and asleep, and tries to seduce her. Disaster strikes. After serious kissing, to which Willa seems to respond, Hilary returns home, convinced a new and significant relationship has begun. Instead, within a short time, Willa suffers a stroke and falls down a flight of stairs. Although Willa survives, she is never the same open, vulnerable person to whom Hilary had originally been attracted (131–46).

Whereas the poetic outpouring that stems from her feelings for Willa is quite good, the sexual part of Hilary's encounter with Willa leads to disaster. Initially a reader may see Willa's stroke and fall as punishment for Willa (and Hilary) having explored feelings marked taboo by society. But Sarton is offering a far subtler critique here, as is made apparent by her letter to Bogan. The problem is neither lesbian feelings nor the expression of them, but Hilary's attempt to initiate an unready woman into a lesbian experience. Willa's illness and accident are thus not indictments of Hilary's love and sexual attraction to women but rather condemnation for Hilary's haste and aggression toward her new muse. If the novel truly condemned Hilary's feelings for women, Hilary would not have had successful relationships with other women in the story, such as her affair with sociologist Dorothea. This relationship, and a later one with Anne, is far less caustic and is thereby less open to a reading that denies Sarton's own lifestyle and interests.

Finally, however, the greatest contribution of *Mrs. Stevens Hears the Mermaids Singing* is neither the aesthetic reflections nor the pioneering lesbian storyline, but the thoughts Sarton offers through Hilary on the self-division experienced by women who strive to be artists. Women who are creative, dominant, and have dreams and desires they wish to explore often find the convention of marriage and child rearing stifling. Sarton reflects in *Mrs. Stevens Hears the Mermaids Singing* that the cost for a woman who chooses to pursue art may be solitude (for a time) and childlessness.

These ideas about the female artist emerge in part when Hilary suggests that men in relationships with women of genius normally seek to "tame" them. The alternative, however, where women artists would themselves take a more dominant role in their lives (and hence become more masculine) results in these women losing something whole and warm in their art (111–12). Hilary suggests that poems and novels of ideas—that is, writing that seeks to communicate some profound intellectual idea or philosophical revelation apart from emotion—is not women's territory. Rather, Hilary maintains, women's greatest contribution to art is holistic and spiritual; women's vision at its best is "never to categorize, never to separate one thing from another. . . . [It is instead a] total gathering together where the most realistic and the most mystical can be joined in a celebration of life itself. Women's work is only toward wholeness" (172).

In what is perhaps the most important passage in the novel, Sarton asserts that women's best writing will represent something whole and spiritual, emotionally deep and intellectually challenging. According to Sarton, then, ideal manifestations of women's art will not break apart experience but integrate it into a new understanding. Echoing chapter 6 of Virginia Woolf's *A Room of One's Own,* where Woolf describes the androgynous brain as that which weds the best of male and female into completeness, it is this nurturing vision that paves the way for the relationship Hilary achieves with Mar (despite its difficulties) and through which Hilary (and Sarton's) writing continues to evolve and grow, even into the recesses of old age. And it is this kind of art that other writers and critics celebrate in Sarton's own work.[4]

CHAPTER SIX

The Relational Sarton
Later Novels

Sarton's novels beyond *Mrs. Stevens Hears the Mermaids Singing* follow her interests in growing older and remembering friends and family who are now gone (interests also reflected in her journals and poetry). In these later novels women maintain centrality and there is a renewed emphasis on what makes and breaks relationships and the family. Finally, in perhaps her most radical move, Sarton imagines in her final novel, *The Education of Harriet Hatfield,* a place that is affirming of lesbians, feminists, gays, and all those who are different from the white Anglo-Saxon norm.

This final chapter on Sarton's fiction will explore these later novels—the more important texts are treated with greater detail and depth than are the lesser ones. The four novels explored in more detail are: *Kinds of Love* (1970), Sarton's study of small-town New England (which parallels her nonfiction discussions of the same subject in her journals *Plant Dreaming Deep* and *Journal of a Solitude);* *As We Are Now* (1973), Sarton's painful look at the holocaust facing the elderly in nursing homes of the 1970s; *A Reckoning* (1978), Sarton's candid examination of the end of life and the value of female friendships; and *The Education of Harriet Hatfield,* Sarton's last novel. The rest of her later novels will be covered in brief detail in this introduction.

Sarton returns to fiction after *Mrs. Stevens Hears the Mermaids Singing* with a novella entitled *Miss Pickthorn and Mr. Hare* (1966). Miss Pickthorn, a spinster and worrier, is confronted by Mr. Hare, a man who moves into a former chicken house located too near, she feels, to her home. Pickthorn must learn love and acceptance as she seeks to resolve this disturbance of her solitude. Sarton here explores the boundaries of her solitary life, once again concluding that a solitude without interruption is loneliness but a solitude that is open to friends and others is enriching and nurturing.

Sarton's 1969 novella *The Poet and the Donkey* offers one of the best insights into her definition and use of the muse—be it person, animal, or otherwise. Her story centers on writer Andy Lightfoot, an aging author trying to regain his creative steam. The reader follows his struggles with a female muse he meets while reading at a university; it traces out her eventual rejection of him and his decision to temporarily adopt a neighbor's mule as a substitute. Sarton here studies the relationship between person and animal, drawing on her experiences with a rented donkey named Esmerelda and forecasting her own turn to animals as muses at the end of her life (seen in her final poetic collection, *Coming into Eighty)*.

Following *As We Are Now* (with *A Reckoning* in between) Sarton explores the issue of rage in relationships in two novels: *Crucial Conversations* (1975) and *Anger* (1982). The protagonist Caro in *As We Are Now* suffers from a rage that literally bursts into flame; yet Caro's rage is directed primarily toward the system and only tangentially toward those who enact or represent it. Both *Crucial Conversations* and *Anger* explore rage directed at another person, specifically one's partner in a marriage. *Crucial Conversations* studies the marriage of Reed and Poppy Whitelaw—at its breaking point. It is told through the perspective of Philip, a close friend of this couple, who ends up seeming a little too close with (and perhaps even codependent on) the life and marriage of Poppy and Reed.

Poppy, who in the recent past has become an artist, is enraged by a life she feels has been lived for others. She comes to realize that the nuclear family and women's art are sadly incompatible; now that the children are grown she has decided to pursue her art and her solitude alone.

This type of rage, however, is more questioned and more potentially dangerous in Sarton's novel *Anger,* which explores the marriage of quiet, solitary Ned Fraser and Anna Lindstrom, a dynamic opera diva who has sacrificed everything for her art until now. Anna's anger dominates the relationship, at times pushing Ned into unhealthy silence and nearly destroying him, their marriage, and her career. Anna must learn that anger can and does have its place in honest relationships but that it must be directed, focused, and controlled or it will become destructive.

These two novels affirm women even more strongly than did Sarton's writing prior to this point. Through Poppy and Anna, Sarton supports women's art, even if it means the destruction or rejection of the nuclear family. Furthermore, she represents women's anger as mostly healthy and as a necessary part of their progress toward wholeness. Representing and accepting women's rage, then, becomes a milestone for Sarton's fiction of the 1970s and the emergent feminist movement.

Sarton's 1985 novel, *The Magnificent Spinster,* reveals a change of pace for her. Here she celebrates the quiet domestic life of Jane Reid, a teacher whose long career has nurtured and sustained many. This novel is a tribute to Sarton's own teacher and mentor, Anne Longfellow Thorp, and presents her most successful example of a character drawn from a real-life relationship.[1] This novel, a sentimental favorite of Sarton's, develops the life of Jane through the eyes of a friend and former student of many years, Cam. The choice to write fiction as opposed to biography is discussed by narrator Cam. Sarton's celebration of the life of her mentor follows in the tradition of a number of disparate journal entries, her memoir *A World of Light,* and two earlier novels.[2]

Kinds of Love **(1970)**

Like the rough landscape which surrounds and infests it, the town of Willard in Sarton's novel *Kinds of Love* embodies both beauty and treachery. Set in a fictional New Hampshire village in the late 1960s, Sarton's thirteenth novel explores the various characters who make up a New England small-town life such as she experienced during the 1960s in Nelson, New Hampshire. The central theme, however, is not just the town itself but how the town brings together two older women and lifelong friends, Ellen Comstock and Christina Chapman. Class boundaries separate these women, often bringing them into misunderstanding, but friendship and the town itself keep bringing them back together.

One of Sarton's most important narrative techniques in this novel is giving the reader passages from Christina's journal at the end of each chapter. Sarton masters the technique well here—much better than with Caro's journal in *As We Are Now* (her next novel), in which this technique breaks far too easily into conventional narrative in ways that probably exceed her protagonist's grasp. In *Kinds of Love,* however, Christina's journals add depth and reflection, bridging the outer world of Willard and Christina's inner landscape. It is also clear through these journals that Sarton has more understanding of a character like Christina, who is slightly more upper class and privileged, than she does of Ellen. Sarton herself came from a class background similar to Christina's and tended more toward Christina's style. Although we see sensitive studies in her journals of this period of "rustics" like Ellen, Sarton still seems to have a closer kinship with Christina and her concerns than she does with the needs of those like Ellen.

Sarton ends *Kinds of Love* at the close of one cycle of seasons, suggesting by the structure and timing that this novel is an open-ended, slice-of-life look at rural New England. At the close of the novel there are a number of unresolved issues: Ellen's despair over her son Nick's condition and her recognition that he may be impaired for years or perhaps never recover; Cathy's pain over Joel's departure; Cornelius's only slight improvement in health; the continuing mourning over the loss of anchor Jane Tuttle; Old Pete's lack of recovery from frostbite and the ensuing amputation; and the class differences that still lie just beneath the surface of Willard. Despite these undercurrents, though, the novel overall offers a nostalgic, sentimental look at small-town life in New England. The novel's strength is that even in the midst of the Vietnam War Sarton could still write a pastoral idyll to what could have been and what might still be.

As We Are Now (1973)

Sarton's 1973 novella follows *Kinds of Love* and adapts the form of a journal explored in that novel through Christina. In *As We Are Now* Sarton charts the last days of semi-invalid Caro Spencer, who is unable to take care of herself and lands in a nursing home. Unable to get along with her new sister-in-law, Ginny, because she too is a woman of will and independence, Caro is dumped at the rest home by her ill brother and his wife. Caro's journals make up the novella.

Sarton draws a comparison between the "disposal" of old persons into nursing homes and the annihilation of Jews and others during the German Holocaust. The Holocaust provides a subtext for Caro's situation, suggesting how oppressed she is in this situation and how someone (for better or worse) adapts to the deplorable conditions of imprisonment. Caro recognizes in the novella that the Holocaust, which caused a universal sense of powerlessness, represents the end of faith in God and humanity. She concludes that this event shows that even in the midst of civilization all have the potential to maim and kill.[3]

Caro's experience in the nursing home shows this potential in her and in her caregivers. The nursing home becomes in Sarton's story a nightmarish netherworld that torments and eventually subdues the old who are discarded there. Caro soon sees, by studying those around her, that "the spirit gets broken" in places like the nursing home because souls live on hope and in the nursing home at the end of life there is no hope, escape, or recovery.[4]

The ways in which the spirit is killed in this environment are numerous and all fall under strategies of dehumanizing the patients: being treated as though they are recalcitrant children; being disallowed privacy for their thoughts; being deprived of enjoying their senses due to the stenches of urine and defecation; being lied to; and being caused to question their sense of the truth and themselves. Caro is subjected, like so many elderly patients, to these processes that have as their ultimate goal her becoming passive and malleable to the will of those in charge.

There are, however, some bright spots that suggest an ideal of nursing-home care that would ensure the health and welfare of the residents in body and soul. This type of care is embodied in Anna Close, a temporary replacement for one of the meaner nurses who leaves on holiday. Anna tries to make the room and Caro feel pleasant: she brings flowers from her garden, decorates the trays that the meals are served on, and really seems interested in the life stories that women like Caro have to share. There is also a pastor, Richard Thornhill, who treats Caro with respect and dignity, and whose manner suggests that he will take action to remedy the situation. Although he does not act in this manner within the scope of the story, Sarton suggests that through him moral reform may be on the horizon.

Caro is so devoid of human connection that when Anna shows an interest in her, Caro falls somewhat in love with Anna. She begins writing about her feelings for Anna in her journals and letters. It is when Harriet Hatfield,[5] the head nurse, returns and invades Caro's privacy and even ridicules her feelings that Caro is pushed into violence. Sarton carefully studies the move from working within the system for change to seeking to destroy the system itself. In Sarton's mind at this time, as is shown through her journals, she was contemplating how African Americans had for so long struggled for change by working within the system and were now (in the late 1960s) turning to militancy and violence. Caro does likewise.

After her personal journals are violated and she concludes that there is no hope, Caro finally makes the turn toward violence and develops a plan to burn down the nursing home. Although she worries about the deaths that will be involved, including her own, she decides it is better to destroy the system than allow it to continue its abuse. Caro carefully plans and executes her plan, placing her remaining journals in the fireproof refrigerator. These are the journals that make up the text of the story.

Sarton, in her darkest and perhaps most profound short work, thus explores the subtle and quiet holocaust that consumes the elderly. Her record of Caro's loss of hope and turn toward violence parallels the rebels of the 1960s who turned from peaceful protest against war and for civil rights (thus working within the system) to violent actions that took them outside of the established order. Caro likewise embodies this shift from working within for reform to trusting only violence to end the problem. Sarton also begins in this novella her investigation into the state of the elderly in care facilities, which later resulted in some beginnings of government intervention. Her novella can easily be read alongside documents like Jules Henry's 1963 study of the condition of nursing homes, which tells of the terrible conditions and dehumanization the elderly face in those homes.[6] The sad truth, however, is that even after several decades of concerned intervention much remains the same in the plight of the elderly. The reader can still visit many nursing homes in this country and find the same conditions Henry and Sarton describe—and maybe within these homes there is another Caro, waiting for the right moment . . .

A Reckoning (1978)

Despite Sarton's ire at critics who pigeonholed it as a lesbian novel, *A Reckoning* is indeed largely about lesbianism. In her immediate response to the criticism of the novel when it was published in 1978, Sarton both affirmed the importance of this novel in her corpus and asserted that it was not a lesbian but a universal novel of female friendship.[7] Perhaps in response to harsh and dismissive criticism, Sarton took to another extreme by refusing to acknowledge its lesbianism. And in fact the novel is not solely about lesbianism; it shows a world of friendship which allows one to openly embrace whoever one is, whether lesbian, heterosexual, or gay.

The central character of the novel is Laura Spelman, an editor at Houghton Mifflin who discovers she is in the advanced stages of lung cancer and has only a few months to live. She begins to reevaluate her life, trying to discover what is most meaningful to her. In the midst of this examination of her life she comes to value what Adrienne Rich would label the lesbian continuum, that is, the recognition of the power of women's friendships.[8] Laura comes to cherish the female connections in her life, analyzing her relationships with her mother, her sisters, and her children. She also is able to help a young writer, Harriet Moers, deal with coming out in a novel Harriet has written against the wishes of her lover and her parents. Finally she recognizes and accepts an intense emotional relationship of years past with Ella, with whom she seeks renewal and reconnection in the face of impending death.

Laura's only daughter, Daisy, causes her to examine the mother/daughter continuum that shapes her experience. At first Laura cannot quite see the continuum: she has not forced her daughter to go against her own sense of herself, as her mother had forced her and her sister Jo to do; rather she has let Daisy have her own way.[9] Sarton represents the tension in this relationship when Laura and her sister Daphne discuss Daisy before Daisy's arrival. Sarton suggests that Daisy's character, though yet to define exactly what she will seek once free, is in rebellion against any form of oppression against self-expression.

THE RELATIONAL SARTON

Closest to Laura's heart and the most problematic for her is her son Ben. As she had in *Mrs. Stevens Hears the Mermaids Singing,* Sarton suggests the tense relationship that exists between a woman who is getting in touch with the lesbian continuum and the gay man who still has not quite found his way. Ben provides another instance of the tenuous bridges Sarton seeks to develop between male and female homosexuals and between family members.

The two relationships that help Laura see her situation with the most clarity are those that have lesbian elements. One of these relationships is with the writer Harriet, who has submitted to Houghton Mifflin what will be the last editorial project Laura takes on. Harriet has just written her first novel, one that, like Sarton's *Mrs. Stevens Hears the Mermaids Singing,* openly explores lesbian identity issues. However unlike Sarton, who always celebrated the fact that when she came out she had no familial ties to worry about, Harriet has parents and a lover who are poised against these revelations. Laura helps Harriet accept her situation and in so doing feels needed and sees the wisdom she has obtained.

Another beneficial relationship involves Laura's estranged girl-hood friend Ella. Toward the end of Laura's life Laura realizes her deep love for and remembrance of Ella. Sifting through old letters, she comes to see that their friendship had meant more to her than she thought. She contacts Ella as the end approaches and her visit with Ella serves as the emotional climax of the novel.

The Education of Harriet Hatfield (1989)

In her journal *Recovering* Sarton provides a telling analogy that helps us more fully understand the issues in this final novel: "What the fear of communism did to destroy lives and to confuse the minds of the innocent to an unbelievable extent under Senator McCarthy's evil influence, the fear of homosexuality appears to be doing now."[10] *The Education of Harriet Hatfield* concerns the growth and development of a woman who is already in her sixties. Having been in a long-term lesbian relationship and relatively protected from the harsh realities that most homosexuals face, Harriet decides to invest her inheritance from her lover in developing a woman's bookstore in a working-class New England neighborhood. What she does not reckon on are the repercussions such a move in such a place will have on her life.

What Harriet wishes to build is a safe haven and community gathering place for women of all sorts. Sarton perhaps has in mind here the kind of women-centered bookstores and community centers that sprang up in the mid-1980s, such as Crazy Ladies' Bookstore in Cincinnati, Ohio, a visit to which she records in *At Seventy* (1984) and in which she had a room dedicated to her. Harriet's store attracts a large variety of women—everyone from the nun Chris and the happily married mother Nan, to the artist Martha, the annoying old woman Sue, and a number of out lesbian couples. At one point Martha compares her bookstore, Hatfield House, to local bars, suggesting that men have always had places to meet and women are now coming into their own.

Although the tenor of some feminism from the mid-1980s to the early 1990s necessarily pushed toward separatism and the valuing of women's unique characteristics, the strain of feminism that resulted in bookstores and places like Hatfield House was not exclusively geared towards the female. Harriet's store is also a safe haven for nontraditional men, such as her brother Andrew, who comes out to her as a result of her store, and Joe and Eddie, two quiet gay lovers living their lives in the neighborhood. Although it is clear that Harriet's traditional brother Fred does not feel comfortable in Hatfield House, there are men who do mark it as a place of acceptance and warmth.[11]

As Harriet struggles with her new identity, she comes to recognize the model she wants to emulate in her elderly friend Caroline. Caroline, who is ill and dying, comes to represent in the novel the ideal for Harriet and Sarton. Harriet recognizes that Caroline is unique and she begins to ponder why. First she notes that Caroline is "open to life," suggesting an attitude of frank honesty and a willingness to encounter what life has to offer. Next she realizes that Caroline withholds judgment on others, demonstrating an openness and acceptance of people where they are—an attitude Harriet hopes will characterize Hatfield House. Sometimes, Harriet suggests, Caroline is even "amused" by that which others would find "shocking." Finally, and most significantly, Caroline exemplifies the values of participation and detachment Sarton had been at some pains to work out in her own life and, in particular, in her more spiritual poetry: Caroline "was an observing participant, and maybe that is rare: to be both involved as she surely was and also detached."[12]

Harriet soon realizes, particularly through the regular visits of Martha and Sue, the cost of being open and trying to provide a haven. While a nun like Chris or a mother like Nan provides comfort and connection for her, Harriet also encounters difficult women like Martha and Sue. This situation parallels Sarton's own struggle with letters from readers (as noted in her later journals), which offer both nourishment and a continuing demand on her time and energy. At Hatfield House Sue proves to be a dominant woman who tends to express herself too vociferously for the gentler Harriet. Harriet also worries that Sue's lack of tact will cause some of her more sensitive patrons to leave Hatfield House.

On the other hand Martha, a frustrated artist, struggles to reconcile her husband's desires for a family with her desire for a career. Harriet initially hangs and sells Martha's paintings for her; however, Martha proves too open and needy for Harriet. When she becomes pregnant Martha comes into Hatfield House to receive confirmation from Harriet for her desire to have an abortion without her husband's knowledge. Harriet is reluctant to endorse this move and when Martha goes ahead anyway, Harriet's reaction suggests her own disgruntlement at Martha's rather selfish decision.

What is most revealing to Harriet, and a key part of her education in the novel, is her realization of the power of class position and money to protect otherwise endangered lives. Harriet comes to see herself as somewhat protected, having lived a relatively danger-free life with her lover. Moving into a working-class neighborhood causes Harriet to experience the danger and hatred that often accompany difference. In her last novel, therefore, Sarton thus tries to imagine what homophobia does to those men and women who experience it and how a sense of community in a place like Hatfield House can ultimately, hopefully overcome it.

CHAPTER SEVEN

Putting Down Roots
Early Autobiographical Writings

In her memoirs and journals Sarton chronicles the life of an independent female artist in the twentieth century. She notes the shift from a Victorian society where women were primarily in the home to women being largely in the work force, the changes in men, and the other results of the feminist movements throughout the twentieth century.

I Knew a Phoenix (1954)

The first of Sarton's autobiographical writings is a memoir that centers on her parents and her life up to the time when she began writing professionally in 1937. The title refers to the ideas of rebirth and rejuvenation that mark her life and that of her family: the family had to flee Belgium because of World War I and Sarton's first vocational choice of a career in the theater fell apart because of the Great Depression. The story of the Sartons is thus a story of surviving and excelling through change.

The volume's subtitle, *Sketches for an Autobiography,* suggests that these writings are detailed, labored, chronologically arranged recordings of her and her family's life. In fact this is the style of the whole. The first two chapters sketch the childhood of Sarton's parents. Sarton's father, George, looms over Sarton's life and text as she begins with remembering her father's childhood home and his descriptions of it.

The more interesting and troubled childhood, however, belongs to Mabel Sarton, May's mother. Mabel's mother and father practically abandoned her at a young age, leaving her with virtual strangers in Wales while they went to Canada. Mabel recalled to her daughter some of the horrific things that happened there. The woman she called Aunt Mollie (one of the two women in whose care she was left) was mentally unbalanced and abused the child. One particularly vivid example is when Mabel was caught as a young child dipping her fingers into sweetened condensed milk, hungry for anything sweet. Mollie's reaction was out of all bounds: she "shook her violently" and "banged the can" of milk "down on the table and forced the child's face on it, again and again, till her mouth and cheeks were badly cut and scratched by the sharp tin edges."[1] Another instance involved a kitten that had been adopted by the family. One day when the kitten had an accident in Mollie's room, Mollie found the kitten and hurled it down the stairs. Surprisingly the kitten was not killed but it did suffer painful injury in its hind legs. Grannie, Mollie's sister and the other woman who looked after Mabel, on that day called a doctor to come and take care of her sister and also made Mollie apologize to the kitten by giving the injured animal a bowl of milk.

There is an interesting subtext to the childhood narrative of Mabel. Sarton remarks that she has found a detailed autobiography written by her mother, but nowhere does her mother's text recall these events. Sarton reflects that while there is no mention of these terrible events in Mabel's narrative, the telling of them had nevertheless left an indelible mark on Sarton's own childhood.

In the section on her parents' courtship Sarton reproduces their letters to one another from that time. This technique creates

PUTTING DOWN ROOTS

an immediacy and, contextualized by Sarton's own writing, an on-the-spot record of their love. Sarton will again use this technique of reproducing primary documents, most notably in her tribute to Matlack, *Honey in the Hive,* but also to a lesser extent in her journals.

The next few chapters describe Sarton's early childhood home, Wondelgem. This beautiful Belgian home represents for Sarton the world lost to World War I. Once the family had a home and roots in George Sarton's beloved country; now, as a result of World War I, they were refugees—first in England, then in the United States. The family's hope upon coming to America was that they could settle down and rebuild the sense of rootedness they had lost when they had to flee Belgium and Wondelgem.[2]

About midway through *I Knew a Phoenix* Sarton turns to herself and her own development. In this second half, entitled "Education of a Poet," Sarton reflects on the long and winding path that led to her becoming primarily a poet.[3] Her earliest and most profound educational experience occurred at Cambridge, Massachusetts, in an open-air, cooperative school named Shady Hill. Agnes Hocking founded the school and headed this experiment through her will and personality. The school was primitive and seen by others as rather tribal. Sarton remembers it being so cold in the main building that the children had to wear mittens while learning to write.

The center of the school was the study of poetry and philosophy. Hocking was the wife of then-famous philosopher William Ernest Hocking and the daughter of then-famous poet John Boyle O'Reilly. According to Sarton, Hocking was "poetry incarnate" and gave the students a sense of the power and magnitude of verse. Sarton describes the school as being made "centrally active" and spontaneous, as Hocking would occasionally break into poetry or prayer in the midst of excitement (104).

Shady Hill caused poetry to become an important and active part of Sarton's life. She developed a stronger constitution there because of the rugged weather, which even existed inside the buildings. She and the other students developed a preference for the contemplative life as opposed to the active because they learned that, no matter what the conditions, the life of the mind could still thrive. Perhaps most significantly Sarton encountered in the school's teachers passionate, motivated, strong female models—not only Hocking but also Katherine Taylor and Anne Thorpe—who would later become models for characters in Sarton's novels.

When she was twelve Sarton spent the winter term at the Institut Belge de Culture Française in Brussels. This school was a radical shift from Shady Hill. More disciplined, more structured, and more believing in rote memorization as opposed to application and individuality, Institut Belge was not as good for Sarton's individual growth. So committed to rote memorization was one teacher at the Institut that the replacement of one word while recalling a section of a textbook meant outrage from her and a black mark on the grade (123–24). Sarton records a residual fear and anxiety about certain subjects such as mathematics and the sciences that initially developed during her time at the Institut.

The high point of Sarton's experience at the Institut Belge was meeting the institution's founder, Marie Closset—a woman and poet Sarton would admire from that point on. Sarton's first novel, *The Single Hound,* was written with Closset in mind. Closset published her poetry under a male pseudonym, perhaps setting up in Sarton's mind the process that would eventually lead to her writing her earliest erotic verse not as a woman in love with another woman but under the disguise of a male persona.

Closset also modeled for Sarton a passionate commitment to art and teaching. Closset never taught a work of art or literature that did not engage her passion and appreciation. Closset's goal in teaching was "enlightened homage—homage enriched by intellectual analysis but rooted in passion" (129). Thus even in the midst of a learning style and environment that often squelched and terrified its students, Sarton found a gem in Closset.

Her experience of high school at High and Latin in Cambridge, Massachusetts, was likewise fairly dismal. In the chapter on this period of her life Sarton focuses primarily on her reading of poetry and her developing interest in the theater. Ironically High and Latin figured most prominently in Sarton's life when she started teaching many years later at Radcliffe and Harvard. She realized that she had developed the same teaching style she had encountered there—a style that emphasized the rules and pushed students to learn them somewhat by rote. She realized that she had become, while still a gentle radical, the same kind of conservative in the classroom that she had loathed at High and Latin.

The last third of *I Knew a Phoenix* centers on Sarton's early and abbreviated theatrical career and her move from the theater into the role of professional poet and novelist. Sarton records her apprenticeship with Eva La Gallienne and the rise and fall of Sarton's Apprentice Theater, which she directed through the mid-1930s. What is of most interest in this section, however, is Sarton's reflection on the ways that her experience in the theater shaped her relationship to writing.

Through her experience with La Gallienne, Sarton learned the effects of submitting oneself fully and completely to powerful art (150). This early submission to art creates in Sarton a passionate surrender to her muse (whoever or whatever that becomes) and to the life of a solitude with an intense commitment to art that resembles a monastic's commitment to God.

Sarton also lists several other attributes she developed in her years at the theater. These include "the sense of what any art demands of its servants, the long discipline in the craft, the devotion, the selflessness, the power to endure" (162). Although she had no formal college education, Sarton characterizes her several years in the theater as valuable in the same way such an education would have been.

After the Apprentice Theater closed in the late 1930s Sarton turned to writing. She records that as a young poet and novelist she had encounters with several significant writers, including H. D., Elizabeth Bowen, and—perhaps most poignantly—Virginia Woolf. Sarton describes in detail one visit with Virginia and Leonard Woolf that occurred shortly after the publication of Woolf's novel *The Years* (an attempt on Woolf's part to be less inward and more relational than she had been in her previous work, *The Waves*). Sarton sees this visit and her chance to know these authors as seminal in the creation of her style and her ambition. Indeed Sarton's first novel, *The Single Hound,* is greatly indebted to and in some sense a derivative of Woolf's writing.

I Knew a Phoenix chronicles Sarton's early emergence as a writer. Never again will she return to the demanding, detailed, rather tedious recording demanded by the genre of autobiography. Although she continued creating biographical sketches in her journals and in her memoir *A World of Light,* they are more impressionistic and less factually detailed. *I Knew a Phoenix* provides the most detailed and significant exposition of her parents' formative years, her childhood, and her time in the theater. Further—and not to be ignored—it declares as its goal the description of the "Education of the Poet" and writer that Sarton had by this time become.

Plant Dreaming Deep (1968)

More a collection of occasional essays than a journal per se, Sarton's next memoir focuses on her move to Nelson, New Hampshire, at the age of fifty-four. Sarton's search for roots, so much a part of *I Knew a Phoenix* and her poetry, finds a home (at least temporarily) in her house at Nelson. In fact in many ways both this work and her first memoir begin at the same place: with Sarton's parents. In her new home Sarton carefully arranges her and her family's antiques and belongings. This care represents her continued connection to the past, which includes Europe in general and Belgium in particular.

Her decision to plant a garden likewise recalls her mother's long devotion to gardening. Because gardens are such an integral part of her journals and writings, it may seem surprising that Sarton never had a garden before she lived in Nelson. Yet chapter 10 records Sarton's first garden, planted with her friend Céline Limbosch. Given that Sarton's first dedication was to her art, it comes as no surprise that she reveals the model for her garden to be Flemish tapestries, small and "intimate."[4] The garden thus brings a sense of belonging and connectedness with the past and the seasons, and (through the return every year of the perennials) a sense of permanence and renewal.

Sarton ends her reflections on gardening by suggesting that gardening is a joy for later in life. Whereas youth is hurried and busy, middle age becomes for Sarton a time of reflection. Sarton for the first time in the journals makes age a self-conscious concern, thinking about the wisdom that comes with being older as well as the problems. There is a new urgency in Sarton's vision as she reflects that her time no longer seems endless, but fixed. She reflects that in order to excel in her chosen arts of poetry and the novel she must not waste any more time (91–92).

The key to redeeming time is to establish routine. As she records in chapter 4, "With Solitude for My Domain," Sarton celebrates routine in this journal. Sarton writes that routine "is not a prison, but the way into freedom from time. The apparently measured time has immeasurable space within it, and in this it resembles music" (56–57). Sarton's reference to music is telling here: the writer must play time like a fine instrumentalist plays a part in a symphony. Otherwise time runs out and wastes the writer's talents and abilities.

To further establish routine, Sarton maintains, one must at a certain level embrace solitude. Sarton celebrates solitude as the place from which creativity and art spring. Solitude "is a way of waiting for the inaudible and the invisible to make itself felt. And that is why solitude is never static and never hopeless." Sarton is also clear that solitude must not be endless or uninterrupted. "Every friend," Sarton reflects, "enriches the solitude forever; presence, if it has been real presence, does not ever leave" (70–71). Although Sarton later reflects that she is not the best of hosts, she recognizes the importance and relevance of friends and visitors at the same time as she resists intrusion.[5]

Plant Dreaming Deep is as much about the town of Nelson, New Hampshire, and New England small-town life as it is about

Sarton and her art. When Sarton moves to Nelson she must first repair the house she has bought. She also has difficulty with water shortages and the consequent digging of a well, which she vividly recounts in chapter 12. Most significant, however, are her encounters with New Englanders as personal friends and as acquaintances within the public sphere.

Sarton celebrates New England folk as "the roses . . . beside the granite" (94), an image that captures their strength, endurance, beauty, and stubbornness. Sarton relates in detail her experience with three New Englanders: Albert and Mildred Quigley, a local married couple who help out around her home, and Perley Cole. The Quigleys are quintessential New England stock with much of the "old world" still a part of their lives. Sarton mentions that she and this couple really talk, and talk deeply. They hold values that seem "anachronistic in the United States," which she articulates as the sharing of ceremony and ritual without competition (81).

Perley also works for Sarton and by his example teaches her the discipline of care and revision. Sarton reflects that Perley is like a man from a previous age, "an age when a workman still had the time and the patience and the wish to do a patient perfect job . . . out of self-respect and out of love of the work for its own sake." Perley's impact on Sarton is so profound that because of his example she "sometimes . . . revised a page a fifth time instead of letting it go after the fourth" (113). Thus the New Englanders provide Sarton with images of strength and endurance that, along with the examples of her mother's and father's endurance, shape a poet who, despite unfavorable or mixed critical reception, will continue to write for love of the art.

The stubbornness also captured by the image of the rose in the granite becomes most fully evident in Sarton's description of Nelson town meetings. Sarton reflects on the frequent battles between vacationers (or "summer people") and townsfolk, recognizing and celebrating the voting process that leads to calm minds and acceptance even from the losers: "I learned the amazing effect, after so much emotion, of the cold, hard counting of votes. Everyone had had his say, and when the ballots were in, calm followed the storm. People who, a few moments before, had flushed red with anger, smiled again, even when their side had proved to be the losing one. This is a small instance of how the democratic way shows its true strength" (167).

Sarton also reflects on the limitations of small-town civic life, thinking in particular about an instance when a baroque group was practicing at a local church. The townsfolk were in an uproar because of the rehearsal noise. Sarton herself enjoyed the music but this instance taught her how little culture is valued by many native New Englanders, and how parochial and closed-minded even the best of New England townspeople can be.

Overall *Plant Dreaming Deep* is a celebration of the civic in New England as well as the solitary female artist. Sarton's quest for roots, articulated so beautifully in *I Knew a Phoenix,* evolves into the decision to "plant" herself in Nelson, and the essays collected in *Plant Dreaming Deep* attest to her strength and determination to go (and stay) deep. Sarton here explores the balance between solitude and friendship, which she seems to achieve during her years in Nelson. Although some would claim that this text idealizes the solitary life,[6] Sarton manages to explore the good and the bad aspects of this life—or, more poignantly perhaps, how the bad can be changed by sheer will into the good.

PUTTING DOWN ROOTS

Journal of a Solitude (1973)

The publication of Sarton's *Journal of a Solitude* marks a milestone in her career and in the overall shape of feminist literature. Immediately popular—in fact still her most popular journal—this text invites the reader into Sarton's intimate domestic world in Nelson, New Hampshire, in a way that goes well beyond the occasional-essay format of *Plant Dreaming Deep*. Sarton here develops a form, perhaps best described as daily essays and reflections, that would become her trademark in several subsequent books.

The genesis of *Journal of a Solitude* directly impacts its form. Sarton had received many adulatory comments about *Plant Dreaming Deep* but had become concerned that the life she depicted there was too ideal and that many young women (and men) might follow her into a solitary life without realizing the pitfalls of that choice. The previous memoir, Sarton realized, had depicted a life that appeared too romantic and abstract rather than presenting to the reader the true frustrations, angers, and bitterness of the solitary life which always accompany the joys: "I have begun to realize [about *Plant Dreaming Deep*] that, without my own intention, that [*sic*] the book gives a false view. The anguish of my life here—its rages—is hardly mentioned. Now I hope to break through into the rough rocky depths, to the matrix itself. There is violence there and anger never resolved. I live alone, perhaps for no good reason."[7] In fact Sarton stands at the beginning of *Journal of a Solitude* in a space rather close to where meaning itself may break down. Sarton affirms even more strongly toward the end of *Journal of a Solitude* that she could not go on living the "myth" that *Plant Dreaming Deep* created because it would stop growth and be a mere imitation of what readers assumed was the real Sarton (143).

Part of the reason for this feeling of impending meaningless-ness is that Sarton had found herself in a rather dry period as a writer. She saw her first truly popular work, *Plant Dreaming Deep,* creating an image of her that she felt was not true or complete. Per-haps most significant, however, is the end of a love affair that had caused Sarton to lose a sense of herself. She hoped this journal would help her find that essential self again and thus perform what she labels in *Recovering* as a "sorting" of herself and a returning to the bedrock.

Several formal innovations result from this attempt to record a truer reflection—a journal—of her life in Nelson. She records day-by-day, trying to capture the direct flow of life as she experiences it rather than remembering it and recounting it more formally (as she had in the essays of the earlier volume *Plant Dreaming Deep*). It is also here that Sarton introduces what would become a characteristic trait of her subsequent journals: frequent references to, quotations from, and reflections on what she is reading. In *Journal of a Soli-tude,* Sarton's earliest journal, one prime example of this referenc-ing—what is more formally called "intertextuality"—is Sarton's detailed reading of psychoanalyst C. G. Jung.

One of the earliest references to Jung comes in the 4 February 1971 entry where Sarton quotes Jung's reflection that the profound-est problems of life are never completely resolved—that, in fact, the time when one thinks they are is perhaps when one is truly endan-gered by them. Sarton concludes from this observation that the prob-lems of solitary life are constantly evolving and not likely to be solved permanently or quickly (101). Thus Sarton continues to emphasize that a solitary life is far from being as easy or neatly rec-tifying as some readers assumed from her previous memoir.

PUTTING DOWN ROOTS

On 13 February she again turns to Jung, this time to reflect on the nature of evil and goodness, and how someone grows from one to the other. She cites Jung's claim that goodness and growth do not come from fantasizing about the ideal but from recognizing and dealing directly with the evils one experiences. Sarton recommends that instead of idealizing solitary life her readers should recoup their own lives to make them good. Another quotation from Jung in the same entry answers the question of how one resurrects the good from the bad: Jung suggests that everyone must first look within themselves and recognize that their struggles originate within (110). Sarton performs this kind of looking within in this journal, modeling for readers the process that will help them become aware of and fix the problems within their own lives.

To further her exploration of the true life of the solitary, Sarton makes a point in this journal to define her solitary status by what it is not. She draws several comparisons between herself and other solitaries, and ends by showing that, while definitely a person of solitude, she is not alone nor unaffected by friends and visitors. Indeed she welcomes them as long as the basic tenor of her life— her solitude—is not disturbed but enhanced.

When she asks herself what it would be like if she were to live a "normal" woman's life with children, work, and a husband, Sarton reaffirms her continued commitment to the solitary life. This questioning causes her to return with gratitude to her solitary life. She suggests in the same passage that she must embrace the "diversity" she is able to bring into her life because variety keeps it interesting and affirms growth (109).

Through references to a letter from a woman identified as C, Sarton reflects that solitude is normally a time of hunger and desire rather than peace and tranquility. Although there are times, according to C, of great exultation, there are also times of tremendous depression and despair. For C, an older female, solitude has become immense and rather terrifying: the friends and neighbors she used to trust are no longer there and her enfeeblement is becoming advanced. Sarton reflects that for herself times of illness are the worst and most despairing. Sarton notes, however, that C's solitude "is far more intense than any I have experienced here," and thus comforts herself by drawing a contrast. Although Sarton vividly describes the fears that affect the elderly who live alone, especially the fear of lying in pain or dead and not being found for hours or days, she is quite clear that her solitude is not as isolated as C's (194–95). In fact as Sarton ages many friends look in on her and later even stay with her for periods of time.

The most famous passage in this journal, while certainly a reflection of Sarton's larger literary goals, more significantly reveals what she wishes to accomplish with this journal in terms of her impact on her readers' lives. Sarton reflects, "On the surface my work has not looked radical, but perhaps it will be seen eventually that in a 'nice, quiet, noisy way' I have been trying to say radical things gently so that they may penetrate without shock" (90). Sarton goes on to reflect on the dangers of homophobia and the courage it took to write her novel *Mrs. Stevens Hears the Mermaids Singing.*

The process of reading any of Sarton's journals, but most significantly *Journal of a Solitude,* is an experience of being gently but firmly prodded to accept new ideas that will, if adopted, lead to a radical change from one's own status quo. From Sarton's celebration of the domestic and her discussion of men's new roles in the home and in marriage to her reflections on the nature of solitude and its connections to spirituality and art, Sarton tenderly pushes the reader into deeper self-awareness. Many readers over the years have taken the implied challenge and started journal writing as an act of self-reflection; some have even started journal-writing groups in honor of Sarton. The current plethora of self-help books that encourage journaling and the popularity of published journals owe their existence to the kind of self-reflection Sarton pioneered, or at very least tapped into, during the mid-1970s.

But Sarton goes even further: she realizes that mere journaling could lead to a kind of self-destructive narcissism. Sarton prods her readers to read other thinkers, challenge their beliefs, and stay in touch with current news and ideas. In the later pages of this journal she repeatedly rejects her readers' idealization of her solitude and announces (to what she perceives to be their shock) her plans to leave Nelson and move to Maine (143–44). This move to York, Maine, would turn out to be the last move of her life.

A World of Light (1976)

The subtitle of this collection of essays, *Portraits and Celebrations,* points to Sarton's goal of preserving detailed descriptions of the family and friends who shaped her life. Thus it forms a counter to her discussion of solitude in *Journal of a Solitude.* It also bridges the gap in memoirs between *I Knew a Phoenix,* which covers Sarton's life up through age twenty-six, and *Plant Dreaming Deep,* which begins when she is forty-five.

Sarton refers to this volume as a celebration of friendship in its ability to bring about change and growth in the author. Sarton again affirms that solitude, while the main thrust of her life now, must be balanced with involvement with others to keep it from making her empty and narcissistic. Excepting one, all the people of whom she writes are deceased. She includes her parents in the volume, seeking to elaborate on the elements of friendship in their relationships with her.[8] Of the persons she describes only two are of historical significance: Irish novelist Elizabeth Bowen and Louise Bogan, poet and poetry critic for the *New Yorker.* The other people Sarton refers to include Céline Limbosch (the model for Mélanie in *The Bridge of Years*); Edith Forbes Kennedy; Grace Dudley; Alice and Haniel Long; Marc; Quig (the subject, along with his wife Mildred, of one of the sections of *Plant Dreaming Deep*); English critic and writer S. S. Kotliansky; and Jean Dominique (the subject of Sarton's first novel, *The Single Hound,* and presented as a formative influence in *I Knew A Phoenix*). While these people are occasionally mentioned in the other journals, *A World of Light* provides a storehouse of information about them that allows Sarton's readers to feel a part of her circle.

Sarton's difficulty in writing *A World of Light* is that she has learned from the journal process she adopted for *Journal of a Solitude* to celebrate the "flux" of daily life and to chart what each day brings, including the particular vantage one gains through reminiscences of others. Writing a "portrait" or memoir for Sarton becomes difficult because of its stable, unchangeable nature. Her return in this memoir to a modified version of the essay form she had used twenty-two years earlier in *I Knew a Phoenix* (and modified in *Plant Dreaming Deep*) prevents her from getting at the essence of the persons profiled—an essence better reached through the less formal and more impressionistic "occasional" portraits of these people recorded in sections of the journals.

The House by the Sea **(1977)**

Sarton's second journal and fifth memoir, *The House by the Sea,* records her life after her move away from Nelson, New Hampshire, and into her final home in York, Maine, by the sea. This home will be the setting for all of the later journals. *The House by the Sea* continues Sarton's reflective recording of day-to-day events. Along with the later journals *Recovering* and *At Seventy,* this journal provides the ideal of a reflective old age, and the sage who is living it is Sarton herself. The journals after *At Seventy* show Sarton's decline and, while there are moments of luminous reflection, never again arrive at the sense of joy, knowledge, and wisdom earned through the years that these three journals do.

Although Sarton does discuss at length the decline of her companion Matlack to Alzheimer's, it is hard to call this journal sad. It affirms the possibility of dynamic positive change, even late in life. Sarton records here the rise in America of a true feminist consciousness which her works have (in part) brought about. As part of this feminist consciousness and by advising on a dissertation by Karen Elias-Button, Sarton explores the importance of recasting mythology from within a feminist perspective. Sarton affirms the importance of an overarching myth of renewal and rebirth, emphasizing that this paradigmatic myth must not merely recast women as superior to men (which would only reverse what men have traditionally done to women), but must become an archetype for a society that embraces the best of both genders.[9] Sarton offers advice and warnings for this new mythology: One must accept oneself as central to the myth, which cannot be imposed from outside of the self. While women are the creators of these new myths, the myths cannot be anti-male.[10] Sarton thus places spiritual truth above gender and embraces the balancing of male and female as the most holistic and complete psychological state for any person.

CHAPTER EIGHT

The Unicorn Grown Old
Later Journals

Sarton's latter journals chronicle her time of diminishment and growing dependence. They are a marvel in their celebration of the wisdom of old age, their charting of ways for a youth-obsessed culture to recover a respect for and admiration of the elderly, and their daily glimpse into the challenges and possibilities the elderly face. From illness and loss and the eventual strength realized in *Recovering* to the despair and grim determination of her last journal, *At Eighty-Two*, Sarton chronicles the life of the elderly in America at the end of the twentieth century.

Recovering (1980)

Recovering, the first of Sarton's later memoirs, candidly looks at the loss of Sarton's beloved Matlack through illness and senility. The various purposes of this journal, which documents Sarton's sixty-sixth year, include keeping herself out of depression, commemorating the end of her relationship with lifelong companion Matlack, and facing the beginnings of the battle with cancer that would eventually take her life. Through it all Sarton shares with readers her experience of losing the last love of her life and facing the death (or at least a change in the nature) of erotic love, which she sets out at length to define.

In the beginning of *Recovering* Sarton explicates the purposes of this journal. She notes that she had not expected to write a journal again until her seventieth year, and she had envisioned that future journal as being celebratory instead of depressing. Yet she admits that during Matlack's illness (the advanced stages of Alzheimer's), she had been unable to sort her life out otherwise. She also notes in this journal her suspicion of the form, suggesting that she places far less value on published journal writing than her readers do. She writes that she finds the journal, as opposed to poetry or the novel, "suspect" because it seems "too easy."[1] And yet, in the discursive space of the journal, Sarton models for her readers the kind of candor she promotes and she charts better and more fully than any other writer the pilgrimage of old age.

In her journal entry from 7 June 1979 Sarton describes how the darker side of the erotic has seldom been explored in Western culture since the Renaissance. This observation leads Sarton into trying to define what this darker side is. She draws a long excerpt from *Eros in Greece,* a book by John Boardman and Eugenio La Rocca which had been included in part in the *Times Literary Supplement.* In the excerpt Sarton culls Boardman and La Rocca argue that Eros was not viewed positively by the Greeks but rather seen as an unruly god who caused chaos and destruction. Sarton builds on this excerpt to define Eros as a necessary "earthquake" in life: "There is fear and trembling and, above all, radical change involved . . . to pretend that Eros is not a primordial being of the same order as Earth and Chaos is to trivialize or screen off what has to be faced and experienced if we are to come into our humanity as whole beings, and to reach Agape" (117).

Sarton struggles here with several issues, at once philosophical and deeply personal. She pulls in a reference to Christianity in the idea of fear and trembling, often used in the Bible and in Christian circles to denote the conviction of sin through the Holy Spirit. Sarton here coopts this notion, suggesting instead that it is the spirit of Eros. Thus she once again recognizes the limitations of Western perspectives, a hallmark of postmodernism she had explored relentlessly since her trip to Asia in the 1960s. This passage also further articulates why the gods that she writes about in her poem "At Delphi" were not happy, but dangerous. These gods embody an understanding of Eros that is far from peaceful and mild. And yet Sarton recognizes that it is only through the route of earthly, physical, painful love that agape—a spiritual, detached, unconditional love—can be known.

Sarton's final comment on agape as the outcome of a full acceptance of Eros comes from her personal experiences at the time with her lover, who had become a victim of Alzheimer's. Sarton deals with an intense feeling of longing and the recognition that life with Matlack could never return to what it once was. She records the experiences of their last Christmas together after a relationship of over thirty-five years, when Sarton had brought Matlack from the nursing home (where Matlack had been residing) to Sarton's home for the holiday. Matlack was distant, unable to participate in any way beyond that of a child. Sarton had to deal with the loss of her friend and companion, and also Matlack's sad decline, which included bed wetting and tantrums. Sarton's heart was unavoidably broken.

As she realizes, it is only through the love she once shared with Matlack—a love that was erotic as well as emotional—that Sarton can now begin to understand what agape, or unconditional love even in the worst of times with no hope of improvement, can be like. She finally labels this age of her life "a Christmas strangely without tenderness" (11).

This loss continues further in regards to one of her last novels, *A Reckoning,* for which she had entertained particularly high hopes. *A Reckoning* had been panned by critics and carelessly labeled a lesbian novel when what Sarton had aimed for was a novel about the enduring bond of female friendship even in the midst of dying. Sarton relates that the reviews seriously distorted the novel and marked what she saw at the time as the culmination of her career. In her 20 March 1979 entry she records a particularly caustic reviewer who claims that her work is all about one theme: lesbianism.

Sarton suffers here from the same kind of homophobia that suggests only heterosexuals can talk about heterosexual experience. Always striving for the universal, often with pain to herself, Sarton rejects the notion that her story and thus her experience cannot account for more than a lesbian speaking to other lesbians. She notes that less than 5 percent of the letters she receives are from other lesbians and the majority of the letters she receives are not concerned with strictly lesbian issues. She writes that what she most represents in the public mind is the role of a "solitary" and that both men and women confide in Sarton about that role (81).

Having lived through the McCarthy era (the paranoia of which she documents in *Faithful Are the Wounds),* she now recognizes a new and dangerous proclivity in modern society: "What the fear of communism did to destroy lives and to confuse the minds of the innocent to an unbelievable extent under Senator Joseph McCarthy's evil influence, the fear of homosexuality appears to be doing now." She further recognizes the double bind she must face as an avowedly gay author: if all her characters are not lesbian, then one reviewer will damn her for lack of courage; whether the characters are lesbian or not, another reviewer will assume they are and damn her for that

(80–81). Either way Sarton's attempt to write that which is applicable to all experience and her quest to find relevance for everyone become lost in the shuffle.

Thus in *Recovering* Sarton grapples with the loss of sexual love in a relationship she has had for many years and the knowledge that (since she came out in *Mrs. Stevens Hears the Mermaids Singing*) she must struggle to avoid having her work labeled by reviewers and scholars as solely lesbian. Yet it is in Sarton's chronicling of the hardships of her life as she ages that her most universal claims to understanding come.

Sarton also chronicles here in her beginning battles with cancer, which lead to a modified radical mastectomy. Although she does not dwell for long on the details of the surgery or her feelings, she gives her readers a glimpse into the battle with breast cancer that will eventually take her life. Much like the last journals of Anaïs Nin (but not as detailed), *Recovering* shares Sarton's feelings about cancer. In her 8 June 1979 entry Sarton writes that she believes cancer comes from suppressed rage, an idea that medical science is now beginning to recognize. She notes that she has always believed her mother's cancer was a result of her suppressed rage bottled for years. Sarton accepts the loss of her breast with quiet endurance, celebrating on the day after surgery the life she has and the flowers friends have sent, once more chronicling her struggle and providing a model of quiet endurance that others can emulate.

Recovering is a raw but tactful journal chronicling the death of passion and the continuing life of the elderly. Easy for readers to sentimentalize, this journal nonetheless acknowledges the stormy undercurrents beneath a placid surface. Sarton talks candidly about the erotic while celebrating lifelong love; she pans reviewers who have panned her; and she comments on the rage that lived at the center of her and perhaps her mother's cancer—all while providing a model of endurance in the face of adversity.

At Seventy (1984)

The central problem for Sarton as she writes her journal *At Seventy* is how to grow older while maintaining grace and dignity. Sarton's search leads her in a quest for models and precedents on aging well whom she can emulate. Although by the end of *Encore* Sarton finds these models in literature, in her earlier foray here she looks to people who have been prominent in her life. In addition to her mother she turns to, among others: Jean Dominique, Lugné-Poë, Camille Mayran, Eva La Gallienne.[2] Through their lives and through the life of Sappho, the mother of all poets, Sarton chronicles what it means to grow old, being, as she responds to a question at a reading at Hartford College in Connecticut, "more myself than I have ever been . . . happier, more balanced, and . . . better able to use my powers" (10).

Although others have followed her model, most notably Grumbach and Heilbrun, Sarton recognizes that (through this and her later journals) she is a pioneer in chronicling what it means to age wisely. For models of aging in this way she looks to both those she knows personally and people in the news. The first important model Sarton discusses is her older, dying friend Eugénie Dubois. Sarton describes her as a woman who "sowed light" in others, especially in her husband who in later years became the kind of companion she needed (58). Dubois considered the positive and the beautiful more often than the negative, even though the negative was so frequently a part of her life.

THE UNICORN GROWN OLD

Golda Meir also provides a model for Sarton. Reflecting on a recent film adaptation of Meir's life starring Ingrid Bergman, Sarton writes that Bergman is far too beautiful to represent Meir. Like Eleanor Roosevelt, Meir, according to Sarton, had a plain face that nonetheless through her wrinkles and age showed tremendous spirit (60–61). This observation leads Sarton to consider that aging and changes in appearance can be beautiful in nontraditional ways if the spirit itself is alive and well.

The discussion of Meir leads Sarton into reflecting on her friend Lotte Jacobi, a grizzled and wrinkled older woman who lives on Star Island. Comparing Jacobi to Meir, Sarton describes Jacobi as "enchanting" and wise (61). When Sarton records a journey to Star Island to visit her dear friend she describes Jacobi as wise and mischievous, still spirited even though quite elderly (72). Like Meir and Eleanor Roosevelt in wisdom, Jacobi also manages to add a sense of humor and playfulness to Sarton's ideal of growing older.

Finally there is Sarton's friend Pauline Prince, whom she describes as a "taproot" for her, bridging her European roots and her American present. Prince had been a literature professor and (like Sarton's other examples) presents an example of wisdom in old age. Prince's wisdom comes from her restorative faith as a practicing Catholic, which also leads her to model modesty and humility even though she is quite remarkable in her intellect and sensitivity (65–66).

Through her friends Prince, Dubois, and Jacobi, Sarton sees modeled the art of growing older with wisdom, warmth, and humor. She also sees this wisdom played out in larger ways in the lives of Eleanor Roosevelt and Meir. Sarton finds her best model in the writings by and about Sappho. One reader's letter, by recalling lines depicting Sappho in Sarton's earlier poetic masterwork "My Sisters, O My Sisters," causes Sarton to reflect on new scholarship into Sappho's work that further expresses Sarton's own belief that Sappho had to practice renunciation—of love and sexuality—in order to achieve greatness as an artist (90–91). Sarton considers that old age is a time of renunciation as one grows dependent and it is perhaps also a time for profound thought and art.

From her newfound strength and wisdom Sarton reflects as a sage on the reality of the mid-1980s in America. Sarton sees her society during the Reagan years as in the process, modeled by the leader himself, of forgetting the poor, the hurting, and those unable to achieve the Republican version of the "American Dream." She chronicles what she considers the ethical and religious decay of the age.

On a national scale Sarton worries about policies that lead to greater endangerment of rare species of animals, and she expresses concern over the health of air and water (59). For example, she notes that people are not only ignoring the health of animals but actively destroying them in cruel and malicious ways. Sarton relates the story of some pelicans whose beaks were sawed off, probably by angry fishermen, causing the birds to starve to death because they were unable to harvest fish (177). The decade of the 1980s marks the first serious recognition by the mainstream middle class of the problems in the inner city, and this is another concern Sarton chronicles (281).

Internationally Sarton registers concerns over the war between Britain and Argentina over the Falkland islands and that war's aftermath (21). She also reflects on the continuing turmoil in the Middle East, brought home to Sarton by a remembrance of her father's pioneering work in science history (work which is still recognized in the Middle East) and the United States visit of a Middle Eastern scholar who came to talk about Sarton's father with her (59).

At the center of that controversial age Sarton places the leader and chief, Ronald Reagan. Sarton's description of Reagan is telling, suggesting that the actor-turned-president knows how to put on a good show with no substance behind it. She reflects on the empty nature of Reagan's gestures toward those seeking justice: "There is never any depth in Reagan's perceptions of the world. He behaves like an animated cartoon, wound up to perform futile gestures and careless witticisms" (21).

Sarton does however note a few signs of hope for the future. One is that the Supreme Court finally seems to be turning in favor of long-disprivileged African American citizens (85). She also sees charity organizations such as Hospitality House (HOME), run by her friends Karen Saum and Sister Lucy, as examples of the kind of humanitarian effort that can change lives one person at a time (127–33).

A darker undercurrent of her age that Sarton witnesses is a denial of history itself and of the Holocaust in particular. She views this forgetting as a symptom of the malaise and apathy of the 1980s as well as a warning exposing a continued anti-Semitism and the danger of a repetition. In her novel *As We Are Now* Sarton's protagonist Caro reflects on what the Holocaust meant to Sarton's generation: "The only thing we could do was to *know*. And after the first shock, and the horror that human beings had done this to other human beings, we had to face that, in some depth beyond the rational, we each have a murderer and a torturer in us, that we are members of each other. All my scientific ideas about progress went down the drain. It was a crisis of faith in man for any thinking person, and, for some, a crisis of faith in God."[3] Sarton's thoughts in *At Seventy* are again haunted by the Holocaust and those who would deny or forget that reality. In this journal she begins to see the Holocaust as the culmination of the hatred embodied by racism.[4] She sees it also as a result of Germany's attempt to remove God from the country by embracing and enforcing atheism (232), although she also believes the fanaticism and intolerance that can stem from religion are just as dangerous as atheism (254–55). At one point she compares the experiences of the Jews in the Holocaust to the experience of a rape victim (301).

At Seventy also reflects on Sarton's state as a journal writer and her role as a chronicler of the age. She identifies her goal as a writer of journals to be "record[ing] a mood as it comes, as exactly as possible, knowing that life is flux and that the mood must change" (34). Sarton writes that at this time in her life, although still seeking solitude, she feels like a runner never catching up; she notes that the journal reflects this struggle (86). Thus the journal reveals the disparity between her ideal (the solitary life) and the reality (her busy social life), as well as the continuing quest to arrive at the wholeness that is the embodiment of the ideal. As Sarton reflects, art at its best seeks wholeness even while recognizing the chaos that is modern American life (105–06).

After the Stroke (1988)

Like its predecessor *Recovering, After the Stroke* illustrates patience and endurance in the face of adversity. Sarton here chronicles for the reader the impact a stroke—even a minor one—has on the brain. Until this point Sarton had not suffered from any incapacity that affected her ability to think and to will. Yet her mild stroke does just that. In this journal Sarton maps her fears in light of the stroke and is drawn to reflect on institutions the elderly frequent (most notably hospitals) and on her beliefs concerning religion and spirituality. Indeed in this volume Sarton culminates her lifelong thoughts on faith and belief.

After the Stroke represents the beginnings of a change in Sarton's style of journal writing; the formal characteristics of her journals constantly change from this point forward and throughout the latter journals. Having developed a particular style of journal writing early in her career, Sarton now struggles with the "rules" she herself has set down. One of her earlier rules that she now discards is to add nothing at the time of publication that was not written at the time of the actual entries. She recognizes that her mind has become impaired as a result of her stroke and that to leave the journal as written would actually exclude readers from experiences instead of helping them to understand. She decides to mark her insertions with brackets, a practice she drops in the later journals even though she continues in them to clarify and revise original journal entries even more extensively than before.

In her entry for 10 April 1986, one of the longest sections in all of her journals, Sarton chronicles her recent stroke and the decline that followed it. This technique of extended narrative of the past (memoir) marks this journal as different from its immediate predecessors and points to Sarton's sudden return to the writing methods she developed in *I Knew a Phoenix* and *A World of Light*. In this extended section Sarton relates (through the original entries and the brackets) what has happened in the past that has led up to her recovery, recording how these events have caused her to live day-to-day.[5]

She records, for instance, the decline and death of Bramble, her beloved cat, due to cancer, which parallels Sarton's own struggle with breast cancer and the stroke. She narrates in detail the events leading up to her stroke: Experiencing strange intestinal pain, Sarton goes to her doctor, who discovers she is suffering from congestive heart failure and irregular heartbeats. The medicine he prescribes for her makes her sick and weak. In the middle of the night on 20 February 1986 Sarton awakens with her left arm unable to move and a feeling of being suffocated. She finally manages to get a friend on the phone. She is rushed to the hospital, where doctors discover the brain hemorrhage that led to her stroke, which may have been a result of her heart problems.

Thus Sarton's journey into the institutions that take care of our elderly begins. Although she never becomes a nursing-home patient like Caro in *As We are Now,* Sarton experiences the hospitals that care for our elderly. Once more she provides a model of endurance at the same time as she recognizes her own weaknesses, both physical and emotional. After being free of the hospital for several months Sarton is once again admitted to York Hospital on 10 May 1986 because she is unable to breathe. Sarton notes what relief she feels once she is given oxygen and can sleep. She notes that while she misses her lovely kitten Pierrot, she is glad to be taken care of in the hospital. Thus Sarton charts the growing dependence of the elderly on others: "I . . . have no wish," she writes, to go home, "only relieved to be here, where I can rest" (43).

Once more, on 24 June 1986, Sarton's doctor discovers heart problems and immediately admits her to York Hospital. Sarton accepts this decision with relish, recognizing that she has often felt unwell and exhausted, even too tired to enjoy her flowers and her kitten. Again Sarton models not only acceptance of dependence in the time of illness, within "the safe cocoon of the hospital" (77), but also the hope that some semblance of recovery and independence can once more be achieved.

The last of Sarton's hospital stays described in *After the Stroke* occurs in a hospice called Philips House at Massachusetts General Hospital. Sarton has here become ill again due to her heart. This experience is far from pleasant: Sarton refers to it as feeling like a "dog in a cage." The disorganization is monumental. Three doctors take her history as she waits in the emergency room and admissions area to go to her room. Even though she is able to walk to a restroom she is nearly forced by one nurse to settle for a bedpan. Sarton is fed food she knows she cannot eat due to intestinal problems. Her friend Maggie is nearly sent away due to misinformation. And Sarton's admission takes nearly five hours. When she asks why the wait is so long, given that Philips House has actually been prepared for her, she is told that she is lucky the wait is not as long as twenty-four hours (102).

Sarton's stay, once in her room, is a bit more pleasant although she notes overpowering homesickness. Unlike her experience in York Hospital, where she was made to feel at home and perhaps was ill enough that the care came as a comfort, Philips House represents the worst in its clinical atmosphere, "bland at best, cold and inhuman at worst" (103). Sarton begins to strive for detachment, trying to contemplate through reading what the effect of this kind of institutionalization feels like for the elderly. She reflects on a passage of a book containing first-hand accounts of hospice care (like that of Philips House), hoping that going home for her will be a return to health and individuality again. Everything about the hospital, hospice, and nursing home, Sarton reflects, strips one of one's identity (102–6). Knowing this—and knowing that she can leave—gives Sarton the strength to return home even though her relationship with home is changing because living there alone is becoming much harder to manage.

Because of Sarton's illness, death seems real and imminent to her. Facing the end of her life, Sarton reflects once more on her beliefs on spirituality. Early in *After the Stroke* she quotes a letter from a biography she is reading about the life of fellow solitary Helen Waddell titled *Helen Waddell: A Biography*. Sarton embraces Waddell's ideas on faith (written in a letter to Waddell's sister), which suggest that love moves the soul closer to God and that to love makes one abide within God, regardless of whether one views this concept through Christian terms or not (78). Personally aligned with this notion, Sarton considers herself to be a Unitarian, a member of a movement that accepts a broad, nondogmatic stance in relation to all religions. She recalls fondly in her journal her experience of attending a Unitarian church when she was ten or eleven and hearing a sermon on entering the "inner chamber" of the soul (152). Again Sarton's faith emerges in relation to her solitude and her inner life, making her faith akin to that of the Quakers but without their doctrinal moorings.

As Sarton faces her end, she sees old age ironically as a type of ascension even though it is plagued by illness and feebleness. Setting forth an idea she will most fully develop in the preface to her poetry collection *Coming into Eighty,* she believes that old age is about the discipline of letting go and living with essences (125).

Sarton's most noteworthy spiritual encounter of *After the Stroke* comes in her visit to a Carmelite convent in Indiana on one of her last poetry-reading tours. Among the solitude and the sisters Sarton finds a stopping and resting place. She finds the sisters' home a friendly, feminine space where she and they can share their concerns, both political and religious (such as, for instance, their condemnation of Reagan's policy in Nicaragua (166)). She compares this institutionalized religious solitude with her own way of life, which is more broadly spiritual and open even to those who hold no religious creed. Being at this convent, however, causes Sarton to realize that she has been "starving for true religious experience" (168). She partakes of the Eucharist with this order, in a strangely open ceremony for an official Catholic mass. Sarton relishes the way the ceremony is conducted, that it is open to her and done in such a way that the priests become coparticipants instead of authoritarian figureheads holding the mystery (168–69).

Thus in *After the Stroke* Sarton once more embraces the solitary life, reflecting on the differences and similarities between her solitude and that of the sisters at the Carmelite monastery in Indiana. She recognizes that her life is not undergirded by traditional religion but is nonetheless valid and able to sustain her even into increasing enfeeblement. She also chronicles the life of the aged, celebrating as well as regretting the enforced institutionalization the elderly face in hospital, hospice, and nursing-home care. Her embrace of the ascension into old age (that for her means a letting go of the nonessential) comes to include her giving up public travel to read her poems and writing, something she had been doing for over forty years. The letting go of this part of her life comes as the climax and end of *After the Stroke*.

Perhaps this idea of ascension is why journal writing itself had by this point become more essential to Sarton. Throughout the 1980s and 1990s (until her death in 1995), Sarton put out more journals than she had in all her years before. This microcosmic look at aging becomes the hallmark of her greatest contribution to literature—a close look at the daily life of the elderly. It also causes her to rethink and reevaluate her opinions about the journal form. Earlier, in *Recovering,* Sarton had dismissed the journal in favor of poetry and the novel, calling it too simple and easy. Now as she grows older and becomes less able to sustain the work that novels and poetry require, Sarton turns to the journal with new fervor and insight. In the entry from *After the Stroke* that discusses Sarton's third stay at York Hospital, Sarton reflects on journal writing at the close of one's life. Reading Frances Partridge's last journal, *Nothing Left to Lose,* Sarton reflects that she hates to see it end. "A journal like this," Sarton writes, "becomes a whole life one lives with, and in it I saw very well that what makes a good journal so moving is not the big events but tea in the garden or its equivalent" (76). In these closing years of Sarton's life the personal and quotidian become the essential meaning and symbols of life. Sarton's life becomes what many writers have noted—sacramental—but, even more so, it becomes heroic. For Sarton now sees and shares with her readers that the act of getting by and channeling endurance into writing gives meaning to life and marks as the true heroes those who survive with joy.

Honey in the Hive (1988)

In the same year Sarton published *After the Stroke* she also published privately and in limited edition a tribute to Matlack entitled *Honey in the Hive.* This work is difficult to come by but worth the effort. Sarton refers to this volume as an "impressionistic portrait" of her beloved friend and companion.[6] This description is an accurate perspective on her own contribution to the volume, but much of *Honey in the Hive* is a collage of writings by Matlack, including poems and a memoir of her father, which may have provided Sarton her model for this tribute.[7]

Sarton has written elsewhere, particularly in *Recovering* and *At Seventy,* of Matlack's decline into Alzheimer's disease and her death. In *Honey in the Hive* Sarton does not elaborate much on this aspect of Matlack's life but instead gives a brief and primarily factual—but passionate—biography of Matlack. While it is certainly worth the effort to find and it is a rare treat to hear the voice of Sarton's beloved through her own poems and prose, it is not considered one of Sarton's major works.

Endgame (1992)

In her writings on aging in *The Last Gift of Time: Life beyond Sixty,* Heilbrun, the longtime friend and literary executor of Sarton's estate, reflects on Sarton's journey into old age. In her chapter on Sarton in this volume Heilbrun speculates: "I believe that if Sarton had not been so ill in her last years[,] . . . if life had not seemed so hopeless, she would have achieved a kind of beauty in old age that was, given her illnesses, denied her."[8] Truly the journals *Endgame* and *Encore* chronicle Sarton's ideals for old age and the reality of living with decrepitude. The journals form a pair: unlike earlier journals there is no interruption between them and no sense of closure at the end of *Endgame.* In fact *Endgame* starts on her seventy-eighth birthday and ends on her seventy-ninth, while *Encore* starts where *Endgame* ends and carries her journal through to her eightieth year.

The prolific nature of Sarton's last three journals ties to technological innovations. Sarton relates that she has begun using a recorder and having a secretary type her entries rather than she herself spending energy she does not have at the typewriter each morning. In her entry for 10 August 1990 Sarton laments, "I have so little ability now to write."[9] The ability Sarton here mentions equates with energy because, due to her multiple illnesses, Sarton has not the energy to type and write at her desk. Only later, near the close of her life, will she completely lose the capacity to write.

The use of this new method of recording her journals has several advantages and once more charts new territory. She can, for instance, write even when she is ill, giving the reader a more intimate glance into all that comprises old age. Further, her style becomes more reflective and discursive. Her entries in the latter journals are some of the longest she ever wrote, due in part to this new method. Once more Sarton had broken ground and changed the shape of the possibilities available to autobiographical writers.

Sarton's decrepitude is the result of numerous illnesses, including loss of memory, confusion, diverticulitis, and intestinal pain, which often leave her unable to write or carry out other usual activities.[10] She admits in the 17 May 1990 entry that she had sworn when she began this journal not to write so incessantly about illness and misery. However the reality of old age and her notable decline in health since November 1989 have caused her to do just that (36).

She admits that the pain she experiences has caused all the walls in her psyche to collapse, making her feel raw and exposed. On 10 August 1990 she reflects that her "extreme weakness" has torn apart any protective barrier between her suffering and that of the world (63). She is haunted at night by images of the Holocaust and of the starving children in Somalia (64). Her pain and the fact that she can no longer easily travel lead her into a close communion with the news and television, about which Sarton provides a candid and on-the-spot recording of her thoughts. Through this disclosure Sarton provides a historical record of an elderly, lifelong liberal's response to the Gulf War and the Bush administration. Readers further get a rare glimpse into the material that will be refined and shaped into the powerful lyrics that make up her final collection of poetry, *Coming into Eighty.*

Sarton's explorations of the Gulf War in this journal parallel and develop her criticism of the Reagan/Bush years in America, a critique systematically begun in *At Seventy.* Sarton first mentions the Gulf War on 20 August 1990 as the military build-up in the Persian Gulf begins. Sarton passionately desires that this conflict not escalate to war and she empathizes with the military men and women caught in the summer heat in desert Saudi Arabia (71). Later in August Sarton reflects that this must seem for the military personnel like "a sojourn in hell" and she states that this war, "like every other war in the end . . . seems so useless, 'stupid'" (79).

Better perhaps than anyone, the housebound Sarton captures the left-wing feeling on the home front as the brink of war with Iraq moves closer. Sarton experiences nightmares, unable to trust our president as having any foresight about where this war might lead. After noting her nightmares and recognizing that war seems inevitable, Sarton raises a series of questions: "When the war starts, what then? If we win, what then? Who knows? Who knows what's going to happen?" Certainly, Sarton concludes, not our "flighty" president (185).

When war is declared on 16 January 1991 Sarton is relieved

that it has begun because everyone has been waiting and knowing it would come. Sarton hopes the war will not escalate to the use of ground troops, where the real "bloody devastation" will occur (209). She reflects (as June Jordan does in her essay "On War and War and War and War")[11] that the billion dollars per day used to launch this war could do so much good for the homeless and the downtrodden in this country. Sarton recognizes and affirms the popular liberal view of the Bush administration that he always shifted his attention to foreign affairs when the domestic needed his attention the most. Sarton's final reflections on the uselessness and devastation of the Gulf War come in *Encore* (which will be discussed in the next section).

In *Endgame* Sarton also begins to question the value of the poet's own feelings, and the lyric form that embodies them, when so much else is going on in the world. In a sense what she is referring to is what poet John Keats labeled the egotistical sublime. Keats maintained that the feeling self in William Wordsworth's poetry was always foremost, creating a kind of narcissistic revelry in one's emotions.[12] Sarton reflects this critique when she writes "Friendship and Illness," her last Christmas poem, in late 1990. Sarton is pleased that her friends have liked her Christmas poems, which she has sent out to a select group each year. However she wonders about the efficacy of writing a "personal poem" when there are more important things happening than "how I feel."[13] Sarton recognizes the need to reveal to her friends through the poem just how sick she has been but she indicts her own lyric as somehow being too personal at a time when a social voice in opposition needs to be heard. This self-criticism leads her to create the political lyrics found in *Coming into Eighty* (identified and discussed in the section on *Coming into Eighty*).

The other hallmark of *Endgame* is Sarton's beginning recognition of the cost of being known. The pile of letters that constantly arrives on her doorstep causes Sarton to feel guilt because she cannot respond to all of them. Watching the letters accumulate, she recognizes that as a writer she has developed a loyal but needy readership and that using her little remaining energy to actually produce more literature is more important and has to be chosen over the drive to respond to fan mail. Perhaps more insidious in her declining state of health are fans who feel it is their right to intrude on an unwell Sarton. A particularly blatant example that occurs at this time is the arrival of a reader named Helena, who intrudes unannounced on a day Sarton is not feeling well. Sarton's vulnerability here is emphasized: Helena brings food Sarton cannot eat, invades her personal space at a time when Sarton is quite ill, and will not go away. Sarton reflects that "this is *not* kindness," but invasion and horror for an invalid writer (247–48). Sarton thus once more exposes to her reader the vulnerability and danger that can accompany someone who is elderly and living alone.

While *Endgame* reflects Sarton's ideals, it more significantly illustrates the reality of being old and ill. Sarton here has lost none of her acuity: her reflections on the Bush years in general, and the Gulf War in particular, are as sharp and philosophical as anything she has written previously. In the quieter moments of the text we find not only whimsy, such as the delight she takes in the long-ago gift of a stuffed duck she still cherishes (182–83), but also the vulnerability, lack of energy, and danger facing an aging solitary. Within these moments, as we read almost between the lines, Sarton critiques her society and then creates a poetry that is purely lyric and purely universal, essentially the political lyrics of *Coming into Eighty*. Rather than portraying old age as a rosy but unrealistic ascendance, Sarton's grim but joyful *Endgame* offers a stirring testament to her life and times.

Encore (1993)

> And where have I been in this journal? Through a
> thicket of ill health into an extraordinary time of happiness and fulfillment, more than I ever dreamed possible, and here it is.[14]

While *Endgame* captures in its moments of deep illness the darker side of growing older, *Encore* explores a moment of health and the return of energy and friends, which sometimes occur in splendid, golden moments of aging. Truly *Encore* is one of Sarton's most positive and celebratory journals, recalling a life that honors who she is and also reflecting more deeply and philosophically than ever before on the art she has created. The closing of *Encore,* with its promise of perhaps one more journal, is one of Sarton's most brilliant and timely explanations of why her artistic life has taken shape and in what directions it has done so. *Encore* celebrates how diminishment in energy and circumference of activity can bring with them renewed clarity and conviction. Much like Ezra Pound's last cantos or moments in the latter volumes of Yeats, *Encore* celebrates the wisdom of the aged and the recovery of health (when it occurs) in beautiful moments of renewed life.

Sarton here continues many of the themes she began in *Endgame.* These two volumes in essence form one long journal and therefore seem rather unnaturally separated. Sarton, for instance, here concludes her exploration of Bush's Middle Eastern policy and the Gulf War.[15] She views with horror the fact that Bush's popularity has skyrocketed due to the Gulf War while his domestic policy has left so much need unmet. What is most important about these discussions for the purposes of this journal, however, is the authority with which Sarton speaks. Sarton emerges here as a quintessential prophet and sage, offering what could be referred to as a jeremiad for her times. She thus rises in *Encore* to a newfound authority in her speech and writing.

Nowhere is this new authority and depth more apparent than in the closing pages of this late journal when she visits Westbrook College for a day which has been dedicated to honor her life and work. Fortunately Sarton is physically able to attend and enjoy one of her last public readings after over fifty years of being a presenting writer. Her health and attitude lead her during this peak of energy into a systematic exploration of her own oeuvre.

In her discussion of this trip Sarton responds to the erroneous idea that the writing and publishing of her journals has revealed all there is to know about her personal life. She reflects that this is not true, that in fact her deep love affairs can only be known through her novels (330). Sarton recognizes here that, because of her plans for publishing journals, certain aspects of her life will only be related to her readers clandestinely through her fiction—if at all. Further she shows that while the journals are committed to honesty, they are also calculated and planned to reveal only so much and they are constructed to explore her image of the solitary, introspective artist.

She reinforces the fact that these journals are honest even though they are written for publication. Many times Sarton has pointed out that she can be honest about herself because her parents are deceased. She feels this offers her a unique and privileged position in relation to her candid self-exploration and also provides her with the challenge to be open where others cannot for fear of hurting family and friends. Further Sarton asks whether poems should not likewise be considered "suspect" because even though they are deeply personal and revealing, they are consciously written for publication (330). She defends her decision to write journals for publication by listing others who have written in this tradition: French writers André Gide, Julien Green, and François Mauriac, and British writer Frances Partridge (330–31). She centers her analysis on Partridge, whom she cites as her mentor in style. She writes that Partridge had an "unselfconscious natural style, which is more artful, I am sure, than it seems. Style in this kind of journal should never show off but rather do as Montaigne adjures us: 'I want to dominate, so filling the thoughts of the hearer that he does not even remember the words. I like the kind of speech which is simple and natural, the same on paper as on the lip; speech which is rich in matter, sinewy, brief and short'" (330–31). Through this discussion of French and British authors, all the way back to an implied comparison with Montaigne's essays, Sarton argues for the authenticity and artistic value of the journal written for publication.

Sarton also returns to the theme of discipline, remarking how the journals have taught her to be honest and candid with herself and her readers. She notes that this honesty is an evaluation of the self "without self-pity or self-glorification" (331). It is no surprise that Sarton's journals have inspired numerous women (and men) to begin journal writing on their own and, also in Sarton's vein, to form groups of mutual support and encouragement for journal keepers. Furthermore, *Journal of a Solitude* is presented as a quintessential model for the prose journal in the latest edition of the *Norton Reader* for first-year college composition. Despite Sarton's earlier disparagement of them, her journals have become her most enduring contribution.

Sarton digresses to explore her poetry and the reasons she writes poems. Again she argues that poetry is about thought as well as feeling and that the poet must discipline herself to strive to find the universal in the particular by thinking hard about her experiences (331). Sarton has used this argument before, positing that form is the discipline of a poem. However here she abstracts further, not mentioning form but instead the discipline of thought about the experience that will make up the poem. This particular paragraph can perhaps be considered Sarton's final summation on her poetry and, in particular, on her understanding of the completed and published political lyrics of *Coming into Eighty*.

Finally Sarton turns away from theorizing about poetry in order to see what she has accomplished in this journal. What has drawn Sarton to think about this particular journal is a comparison of it with poetry: "'My poems teach me where I have to go,' is a line from a famous poem of Theodore Roethke's. The journal tells me where I have been" (331). Sarton's journey through *Endgame* and *Encore* is one from pain to recovery, from diminishment to clarity. She writes that this journal, and the previous *Endgame*, have chronicled her journey "through a thicket of ill health into an extraordinary time of happiness and fulfillment . . . [in] my old age, the recognition I longed for, a rare kind of love shared with Susan, and even enough money to be able to give a lot away! But far more reason for happiness even than these, the sovereign reason that I am writing a poem almost every day" (331).

Sarton's creative prowess has returned. She optimistically fore-casts a new collection of poems, a novella, and perhaps a journal of her eighty-fifth year, but she also acknowledges that *Encore* may be her last (331). She thus recognizes her frailty and the rapidly elaps-ing time she has left in her life for writing. Although the only publi-cation that will postdate *Encore* is her last journal, *At Eighty-Two,* Sarton shares her optimism and the promise that being elderly does not preclude one from enjoying a full, joyful, and creative life.[16]

At Eighty-Two (1996)

Sarton's final journal, published posthumously but edited by her before her death in 1995, is a recognition and celebration of "real old age."[17] Sarton's struggles throughout her final years are vividly and candidly recorded. Although much of the tone of *At Eighty-Two* marks this journal as a time of depression for the author, what remains remarkable is the way that, against all odds, Sarton manages to continue to strive and fight for the best that old age has to offer.

Sarton's friend Heilbrun, in *The Last Gift of Time,* reflects on what those last years for Sarton were like:

> By the end, I too wished for her death; she was so miserable, unable to perform even the simplest house-hold chores without extreme fatigue, above all, unable to write or even compose poems in her head. I believe her doctors thought hers were the problems of old age and couldn't be helped, and she was grateful for their opinions. They quite clearly believed her life was ending, and that there was nothing to be done.

> She was afflicted with many ailments—strokes, can-
> cerous fluids in her lungs, a congestive heart condi-
> tion, irritable bowel syndrome—each sufficient to kill
> a less vibrant person.[18]

Sarton's vibrancy as well as her decline come through clearly in this last journal. Many of the characteristics of the earlier journals are here: her reflections on poetry and reading; her continuing engagement with the political landscape of the time; and her love of nature, animals, and friends. However *At Eighty-Two* also turns remarkably inward as Sarton's actions and lifestyle become more restricted as her illness increases.

Due in a large part to her growing frailty, Sarton again makes an innovation in her journal style. As she mentions in her author's note, she has silently annotated the recorded entries so that when there is needed background or additional insights she can give them.[19] Thus some the entries are longer and more involved and are perhaps read a little more like essays than those of her other journals.

Sarton at first desires to call this journal *kairos,* a Greek word she defines as "a unique time in a person's life; an opportunity for change" (11). *At Eighty-Two* marks a time of radical change and diminishment for her. Sarton recognizes towards the beginning of this journal that she has been gearing-up her entire life for the challenges of "real old age" (27). In the opening pages Sarton reflects that the structures she has built up over the years, including her daily routine, have recently been sustaining for her but have taken a beating. She recognizes that her energy level is often spent carelessly, such as in waiting for a friend who arrives late, and that even petty irritations can drain her of all she might otherwise accomplish in a day (15). As she quotes Shakespeare's *Richard II* at one point, "I wasted time, and now doth time waste me" (57).

Sarton's final volume of poetry, *Coming into Eighty,* is at this time in the final stages of revisions and additions, and Sarton reflects on the nature of her poetry and of lyric in general. Sarton looks to her precursors in the lyric, remarking that pure lyric "is never in fashion and never out of fashion" (26). She cites A. E. Housman and Frances Cornford, and makes references to Louise Bogan, as she reflects that lyric poems are powerful and memorable, covering all aspects of life, from the "passionate" and "explosive" to the "ironic" and "elegaic" (26). She hopes that lyric in general and hers in particular will be read aloud, thus affirming its musical quality as well as its capability of building community among readers and listeners (29). She celebrates when an interview is a real pleasure and laments when one is a real strain, and finally recognizes once more that she has not received the critical attention she feels she has deserved.

Sarton continues to watch and react to the political scene of the mid-1990s. She favors Clinton and hopes he gets the help he needs to accomplish what he desires. She also remains troubled by the legacy of the Holocaust and believes there is a similar event occurring in Bosnia. Sarton feels "haunted" by this reality and warns readers that even though we know what is going on—the news presents pictures of the genocide daily—we seem to be doing nothing to stop it.[20] In fact because of the media Sarton feels as though the reality of these horrible events is constantly bombarding her mind (119–20).

At the same time and as a response to personal and national crises, Sarton longs for but cannot obtain religious consolation. She admires Grumbach, whose two journals, *Coming into the Endzone* and *Extra Innings*, provide a subtext and comparison for Sarton's final journals. Sarton recognizes that Grumbach's faith as a Catholic gives her a level of confidence and a place to turn when times get hard, such as when her daughter faces surgery (109). Sarton reflects that for herself, however, this consolation seems deceptive and that her beliefs, which have developed over a lifetime, do not allow her that refuge.

Sarton's respect for, rejection of, and paradoxical yearning for the more conventional religious life comes through in these reflections on Grumbach. Sarton writes that she "envies [Grumbach] that certainty, that belief that praying . . . helps. I have always thought that praying mostly helped the person who prays and that perhaps that was the point of it. But then I think of all the people who have said that they prayed for me, and how grateful I always am at the idea that they are thinking of me and lifting me up in their thoughts" (109). Sarton further elaborates on this connection between prayer and the self in another entry concerning Grumbach. Again Sarton chooses the term "envy" to describe her feeling about others' certainty of belief: "Prayer is extremely valuable and should be done as much as one can although I do not believe in a personal God. I think what prayer does is to lift one out of the extremely personal into some larger sphere where one is a little more than oneself, and where one feels, perhaps, part of a greater universe" (120). Thus Sarton relates one final time what constitutes her relationship to faith in general and orthodox Christianity in particular. As Sarton's own strength diminishes, she faces her own mortality and explores her beliefs concerning God and prayer, finding herself longing for that personal relationship with God but at the same time remaining on what for her has become shaky, fearful ground by rejecting it once more.

As Sarton moves closer to her own end, she is constantly aware of the threat of illness and the reoccurrence of cancer, which has been in remission since her mastectomy.[21] She also recognizes moments when she has little strokes and when she is quite forgetful or cannot form the right word. Thus occasionally in this final journal Sarton covers a topic twice, saying practically the same thing again. In facing the prospect of her own death Sarton reflects poignantly that "the death wish is rather strong." However at the same time she celebrates perfect moments that come even in the midst of grave illness: "having one day to myself . . . lifted my spirits beyond absolute despair, and now I have another day here alone with no appointments and it does seem like heaven."[22]

Thus the key to understanding and appreciating this final journal is Sarton's recognition that she has now entered what she labels "real old age." As Sarton has pointed out before, she has outlived the life span of both of her parents. Her lack of energy and continuing illnesses make the moments of true sweetness rare and all-consuming when they occur. Sarton continues the process of learning when to let go and when to celebrate and expend her energy, such as in seeing her only play, *The Music Box Bird,* finally produced.[23]

The moments of celebration finally belie Sarton's own assertions of her inadequacy. Although she ends the journal with some reflections on her own incapacity, seeing herself as merely "an old woman living alone,"[24] Sarton manages once more to embrace hope in the face of despair and pleasure amid pain. Perhaps Sarton's greatest legacy is her sensitive chronicling of growing older and her recording that even in the worst of circumstances, and without the foundation of traditional religious belief, one can still overcome and move into the golden years weary but hopeful.

Chapter One—Understanding May Sarton

1. May Sarton, *Endgame: A Journal of the Seventy-Ninth Year* (New York: W. W. Norton, 1992), 80.

2. This theme can be seen most clearly in Sarton's novels, particularly in *Crucial Conversations* (New York: W. W. Norton, 1975) and *Anger* (New York: W. W. Norton, 1982), in which anger and other harsh emotions become central to the relationships described.

3. Sarton, *Recovering: A Journal* (New York: W. W. Norton, 1980), 146.

4. Sarton, *Selected Letters, 1916–1954,* ed. Susan Sherman (New York: W. W. Norton, 1997), 318–19.

5. Paula G. Putney, "Sister of the Mirage and Echo: An Interview with May Sarton," in *Conversations with May Sarton,* ed. Earl G. Ingersoll (Jackson: University Press of Mississippi, 1991), 4.

6. Perhaps we can best see the problems and perils of a relationship with Sarton by looking at her lifelong friendship with the poet Louise Bogan. For an analysis of this relationship, see Elizabeth Evans, *May Sarton Revisited* (Boston: Twayne, 1989), 13–18.

7. Sarton, *I Knew a Phoenix: Sketches for an Autobiography* (New York: W. W. Norton, 1954), 121.

8. Ibid., 148.

9. Ibid., 150.

10. For all but the last item of this selected listing of the most important honors and awards Sarton received, I am indebted to Earl G. Ingersoll (*Conversations,* xx–xxii).

11. Sarton, *After the Stroke: A Journal* (New York: W. W. Norton, 1988), 272.

12. Stephen Robitaille, "Writing in the Upward Years: May Sarton, Zen, and the Art of Aging," in *A Celebration for May Sarton:*

Essays, ed. Constance Hunting (Orono, Maine: Puckerbush Press, 1994), 58.

13. Sarton, *Recovering,* 36.

14. Ibid.

15. Barbara Bannon, "May Sarton," in *Conversations,* 18.

16. Sarton, *Recovering,* 45.

17. Ibid.

18. Sarton, *Halfway to Silence: New Poems* (New York: W. W. Norton, 1980), 50.

19. Sarton, *Recovering,* 13.

20. Carolyn G. Heilbrun, *Reinventing Womanhood* (New York: W. W. Norton, 1979), 65. Heilbrun refers to liberation specifically for women but it also applies to true liberation no matter what one's gender, race, or background.

21. Sarton, *Endgame,* 248–49.

22. Martha M. Gordon, "An Impossible Creature," *Nation,* 30 June 1997, 29.

23. This criticism is not original and merely summarizes the tenor of the majority of reviews of Peters's biography.

24. Sarton, *Halfway to Silence,* 44.

25. Evans, *May Sarton Revisited,* 113.

26. Heilbrun, "The May Sarton I Have Known," in *Celebration,* 9.

27. Sarton, *Recovering,* 81.

28. Sarton, *Halfway to Silence,* 55.

29. Ibid., 43.

30. Ibid.

31. Sarton, *Recovering,* 33.

32. Ibid., 115.

33. Ibid., 117.

34. Sarton, *Halfway to Silence,* 20.

35. Sarton, *Phoenix,* 162.

36. For an interesting study of Sarton's search for belonging and her acquisition of at least one place of belonging in Maine, see Phyllis F. Mannocchi, "'Growing into Solitude': May Sarton's Maine Landscape," in *Celebration,* 25–47.

Chapter Two—In Search of Essence: Early Poetry

1. For a discussion of why lyric poetry is often produced by writers with an excess of emotion, see Christian Wiman, "Finishes: Notes on Ambition and Survival," *Poetry* 169, no. 3 (1997): 222–24.

2. See Sarton, "The Writing of a Poem," in *Writings on Writing* (Orono, Maine: Puckerbush Press, 1980), 44.

3. See particularly *Conversations,* ed. Ingersoll, 58, 171.

4. The status of the relationship depicted in the early sonnets is biographically clear as lesbian love but complex in regards to Sarton's self-conception. In a 1991 interview Sarton admits that she wrote these early poems "as . . . a young man." She suggests that she did not think of herself fully as a woman loving another woman in her love poems until after age forty (Marilyn Kallet, ed., *A House of Gathering* [Knoxville: University of Tennessee Press, 1993], 25). This realization would date from *The Land of Silence* (New York: Rinehart, 1953) and most notably in her early poetry of the sonnet sequence "A Divorce of Lovers" from *Cloud, Stone, Sun, Vine* (New York: W. W. Norton, 1961).

5. Sherman, ed. *Selected Letters,* 77. For additional details of their relationship, see Margot Peters, *May Sarton: A Biography* (New York: Alfred A. Knopf, 1997), 61–64.

6. May Sarton, *Collected Poems, 1930–1993* (New York: W. W. Norton, 1993), 26.

7. Ibid., 27.

8. Ibid., 32.

9. Stephens's quest for the pure is similar in intent at least to Sarton's own quest for the universal; she will later conceive of it in similar terms.

10. Sarton, *Collected Poems,* 48.

11. Sarton, *Selected Letters,* 143.

12. Sarton, *Collected Poems,* 42. "Memory of Swans" begins to move away from the traditional sonnet meter of iambic pentameter into more experimental line lengths.

13. Sarton may be fearing here that the hard form of the sonnet does not register the intensity of the grief, thus suggesting the limits of her reliance on form to shape emotion into a reasoned art.

14. Sarton's references to nettles and flowers in this sequence may be inspired by the very similar symbolism found in Edna St. Vincent Millay's earlier volume *A Few Figs from Thistles.*

15. Sarton, *Collected Poems,* 37.

16. Ibid., 38.

17. There is some discussion of Yeats's influence on Sarton's work in Catherine B. Emmanuel's "'Sailing' to a Different Shore: Sarton's Revisioning of Yeats," in *Celebration,* 79–87.

18. This same turn away from Europe and toward America occurs concurrently in her novel *The Shadow of a Man* (New York: W. W. Norton, 1950), which can be read as a companion to this move in the poetry of this volume.

19. Sarton, *Selected Letters,* 170.

20. Sarton, "The Writing of a Poem," 43.

21. Ibid., 44.

22. In a 1977 interview Sarton refers to this subconscious in the words of C. J. Jung as the "collective unconscious." See Karla Hammond, "To Be Reborn: An Interview with May Sarton," in *Conversations,* 35.

23. Not all of Sarton's verse on the South is as positive. Indeed "Winchester, Va." seems a high point in her conception of the South as consisting of an otherwise dead or dying landscape and a people who refuse to acknowledge the sins of their past. See, for instance,

"Charleston Plantation" and "Where the Peacock Cried" (*The Lion and the Rose* [New York: Rinehart, 1948], 17–19) for more dismal views of the South and the legacy of slavery.

24. David Bradt, "A Conversation with May Sarton," in *Conversations*, 203.

25. I am closely paraphrasing Elaine Showalter's reading of Teasdale's poem; see *Sister's Choice: Tradition and Change in American Women's Writing* (New York: Oxford University Press, 1994), 108–9.

26. Sarton, *Collected Poems*, 80.

27. Dolores Shelley, "A Conversation with May Sarton," in *Conversations*, 68.

28. Sarton initially published some of the poems included in her 1953 volume *The Land of Silence* as a small chapbook, which was printed by Cornell College in 1950 and entitled *The Leaves of the Tree*. She returns to this designation of two separate volumes in the collected poems. My discussion treats the poems in them together.

29. Sandra M. Gilbert and Susan Gubar, *No Man's Land: The Place of the Woman Writer in the Twentieth Century*, vol. 1, *The War of the Words* (New Haven: Yale University Press, 1988), 213.

30. For another example of this pursuit of a different mode of time, see Sarton's poem "Now I Become Myself," in *The Land of Silence* (New York: Rinehart, 1953), 162.

31. Hammond, "To Be Reborn," 35.

32. See Robitaille, "Writing in the Upward Years," 57–67.

33. See Richard J. Foster, *Streams of Living Water: Celebrating the Great Traditions of Christian Faith* (San Francisco: Harper San Francisco, 1998), 235–74.

34. See Kenneth Burke, introduction and chap. 1 in *The Rhetoric of Religion: Studies in Logology* (Berkeley: University of California Press, 1961).

35. For further explication of Sarton's definition of prayer, see her poem "Letter to an Indian Friend," in *The Land of Silence*, 138.

36. Renée Curry, "May Sarton and Elizabeth Bishop: Women Certain of a Revisionist Age," in *Celebration,* 241.

37. Curry, "May Sarton and Elizabeth Bishop," 243.

38. See Patricia S. Yaeger, *Honey-Mad Women: Emancipatory Strategies in Women's Writings* (Columbia: Columbia University Press, 1988).

39. Sarton, *Collected Poems,* 181, 189.

40. Sarton, *Among Usual Days: A Portrait,* ed. Susan Sherman (New York: W. W. Norton, 1993), 165. Sarton relates her and her mother's visit to Muzot in a letter to Juliette Huxley dated 13 July 1948. For Sarton's view that Rilke is her ideal as a poet, see her 18 December 1938 letter to S. S. Kotliansky, *Among Usual Days,* 193.

41. Sarton, *Collected Poems,* 207.

42. See Peters, *May Sarton,* 241.

43. We see this search and its cost most strongly in her invocation to the angels to guide her in her opening poem to this volume, "The Beautiful Pauses," in *A Private Mythology* (New York: W. W. Norton, 1966), 13.

44. Sarton, *Collected Poems,* 252.

45. In classical mythology Pallas Athena most often represents wisdom, but she occasionally signifies military might and female empowerment.

46. In the collected poems "Islands and Wells" is listed in the section entitled *The Leaves of the Tree.*

Chapter Three—The Sage Emerges: Later Poetry

1. The cave is a standard image for the womb and thus female interiority.

2. Peters, *May Sarton,* 266.

3. Virginia Woolf, *A Room of One's Own* (San Diego: Harcourt Brace Jovanovich, 1929), 98.

4. Sarah Ban Breathnach, *Simple Abundance: A Daybook of Comfort and Joy* (New York: Warner Books, 1995).

5. The cat mentioned here is most likely inspired by Bramble, who came to her as a wild cat desiring food and love and became a companion and pet.

6. Sarton traces her own recovery through psychotherapy in the poem "The Action of Therapy," in *Collected Poetry,* 407–12.

7. For a facsimile version of two drafts of the poem "Old Lovers at the Ballet," see *House of Gathering,* ed. Kallet, 113–14.

8. Emanuel, "Sailing to a Different Shore," in *House of Gathering,* 116. Subsequent references are given parenthetically in the text.

9. Sarton, *Collected Poems,* 457.

10. See Peters, May Sarton, 214.

11. Bobby Caudle Rogers, "Imagining the Unicorn: Poetic Sequence in May Sarton's Letters from Maine," in *House of Gathering*, 99.

12. Jane Miller, "In the Simple Day: A Foray into May Sarton's Poetry," in House of Gathering, 177.

13. Rogers, "Imagining the Unicorn," 103.

14. Sarton, *Collected Poems*, 464. The Nootka were a northwest Pacific tribe known for their prowess in hunting within that rugged territory as well as for their rich musical heritage. See "Nootka," Encyclopedia Britannica Online http://www.eb.com:180/bol/topic?eu=57494&sctn=1

15. Rogers, "Imagining the Unicorn," 101.

16. Sarton, *Collected Poems*, 465.

17. See Rogers, "Imagining the Unicorn," 97.

18. Ibid., 106.

19. For a discussion of this relationship as depicted in the journals, see my discussions of *Recovering* and *At Seventy.*

20. Sarton, *Collected Poems*, 489.

21. See Luke 1:46–55.

22. See Peters, May Sarton, 116–18, 130.

23. Sarton, *Collected Poems,* 505.

24. Matt. 5:5.

25. For a theoretical look at the kind of silence and compassion that can lead to revolution, see bell hooks, *Teaching to Transgress: Education as the Practice of Freedom* (New York: Routledge, 1994), 174.

26. Sarton, *Encore* (New York: W. W. Norton, 1993), 331.

27. Sarton, *Coming into Eighty* (New York: W. W. Norton, 1994), 11.

28. Ibid., 11.

29. For details on Pierrot's arrival and his early days with Sarton, see *After the Stroke,* 24ff.

30. Sarton, *Coming into Eighty,* 12.

31. Adrienne Rich, "'Sliding Stone from the Cave's Mouth,'" *American Poetry Review* (September–October 1990): 12.

32. Sarton, *Encore,* 95.

Chapter Four—From Europe to America: Early Novels

1. Sarton recounts her encounters with Dominique in several chapters of *I Knew a Phoenix.*

2. Many readers have noticed a comparison between Cavan and Professor F. O. Mathiessen. However, Sarton denied that she deliberately based Cavan on him.

3. Sarton, *The Small Room* (New York: W. W. Norton, 1961), 249.

Chapter Five—Philosophical Reflections at Midlife: *Mrs. Stevens Hears the Mermaids Singing*

1. For detailed discussions of their relationship over many years, see Peters, *May Sarton,* 198, 224, 245–46, and Elizabeth Frank,

Louise Bogan: A Portrait (New York: Alfred A. Knopf, 1985), especially chapters 9 and 11.

2. Sarton, *Selected Letters,* 344–45. Subsequent references are given parenthetically in the text.

3. Sarton, *Mrs. Stevens Hears the Mermaids Singing* (New York: W. W. Norton, 1965), 16. Subsequent references are given parenthetically in the text.

4. See for instance Janet Catherine Berlo, "The Artist and Her Domestic Muse: May Sarton, Miriam Shapiro, Audrey Flack," in *That Great Sanity: Critical Essays on May Sarton,* ed. Susan Swartzlander and Marilyn R. Mumford (Ann Arbor: University of Michigan Press, 1992), 85–108.

Chapter Six—The Relational Sarton: Later Novels

1. As has been noted, several of Sarton's characters have been a direct result of her desire to pay tribute to a former friend or mentor. The earliest of these is the character Dorothée Latour in Sarton's first novel, *The Single Hound,* who resembles Sarton's mentor Jéan Dominique. Another is her weakest tributary character, Mélanie Duchesne in *The Bridge of Years,* whom Sarton models after Céline Limbosch. Sarton's strongest tributary character is Jane Reid in *The Magnificent Spinster,* whom Sarton developed as a tribute to her teacher and mentor Anne Longfellow Thorp. While there are others, these are the three most important characters offered in tribute to someone specific from Sarton's life.

2. See note 1 on *The Magnificent Spinster.*

3. Sarton, *As We Are Now* (New York: W. W. Norton, 1973), 42–43.

4. Sarton, *As We Are Now,* 53.

5. Oddly, not related to Sarton's title character in her final novel, *The Education of Harriet Hatfield* (New York: W. W. Norton, 1989).

6. Jules Henry, "Human Obsolescence," in *Against the Current: Readings for Writers,* ed. Pamela J. Annas and Robert C. Rosen (Upper Saddle River, N.J.: Prentice Hall, 1998), 76–88.

7. For Sarton's response to the criticism, which is recorded in *Recovering,* see my discussion of this journal in chapter 8.

8. Adrienne Rich, "Compulsory Heterosexuality and Lesbian Existence," *Signs* 5, no. 4 (1980): 648.

9. Sarton, *Reckoning,* 33.

10. Sarton, *Recovering*, 80.

11. Sarton has not by this point, though, grown much in her depiction of male homosexuality. She still (as in the early letter discussed in the chapter on Mrs. Stevens) sees male homosexuality primarily in sexual terms; as the impending fate of Eddie suggests, Sarton is both realistic about the cost of not embracing monogamy in gay relationships and still a bit reluctant to accord gay men the same kind of spirituality she grants lesbians.

12. Sarton, *The Education of Harriet Hatfield* (New York: W. W. Norton, 1989), 188.

Chapter Seven—Putting down Roots: Early Autobiographical Writings

1. Sarton, *Phoenix,* 31–32.

2. Sarton, *Phoenix,* 84–85. This flight accounts for Sarton's search for roots and perhaps, by extension, the plant imagery found in many of her writings. Subsequent references are given parenthetically in the text.

3. Even the title of this section marks Sarton's belief that she is primarily a poet even though by the time she had written *Phoenix* she had published several novels.

4. Sarton, *Plant Dreaming Deep* (New York: W. W. Norton, 1968), 121. Tapestries are also celebrated in her early poem "The Lady and the Unicorn," in *Collected Poems,* 84. Subsequent references to *Plant* are given parenthetically in the text.

5. Sarton, *Plant,* 157. Regarding her questionable hosting skills, most of her close friends recognized—and her biographer Peters excoriates Sarton for—this aspect of her personality. For a sympathetic but candid view of Sarton as hostess and friend, see Heilbrun, *Last Gift of Time: Life beyond Sixty* (New York: Ballantine Books, 1997), 86–88.

6. And this charge would be the impetus to record her daily struggles and triumphs in her next memoir, *Journal of a Solitude* (New York: W. W. Norton, 1973).

7. Sarton, *Solitude,* 12. Subsequent references are given parenthetically in the text.

8. Sarton, *A World of Light: Portraits and Celebrations* (New York: W. W. Norton, 1976), 13.

9. For Sarton this myth is the story of the phoenix, who rises from its ashes again and again. In fact Sarton commissioned from artist (and landlord) Beverly Hallam a stone sculpture of a phoenix, which she then displayed in her garden. This representation is photographed on page 246 of the volume *The House by the Sea.*

10. Sarton, *The House by the Sea* (New York: W. W. Norton, 1977), 224–25.

Chapter Eight—The Unicorn Grown Old: Later Journals

1. Sarton, *Recovering,* 45. Subsequent references are given parenthetically in the text.

2. Sarton, *At Seventy,* 11–12, 111, 227–28. Subsequent references are given parenthetically in the text.

3. Sarton, *As We Are Now*, 42–43.

4. Sarton, *At Seventy*, 150. Subsequent references are given parenthetically in the text.

5. Sarton, *After the Stroke*, 19. Subsequent references are given parenthetically in the text.

6. Sarton, *Honey in the Hive: Judy Matlack 1898–1982* (Boston: Warren Publishing, 1988), 1.

7. It also is very similar in content and style to Sarton's own collection of tributes, *A World of Light*.

8. Heilbrun, *Last Gift of Time*, 86–87. In a recent conversation with me at the Modern Language Association on the evening of 28 December 1999, Heilbrun mentioned that she views this candid chapter (and a few other comments on Sarton made in this text) as a response to the exposé quality of Peters's biography; but she also noted that these comments were actually written before the biography was published.

9. Sarton, *Endgame*, 63.

10. Sarton, *Endgame*, 36, 37, 55. Diverticulitis is a gastrointestinal disorder which often causes abdominal pain. Subsequent references to *Endgame* are given parenthetically in the text.

11. June Jordan, "On War and War and War and . . . ," in *Against the Current: Readings for Writers*, ed. Pamela J. Annas and Robert C. Rosen (Upper Saddle River, N.J.: Prentice Hall, 1998), 611–15, 612.

12. I am referencing here the critique of Wordsworth Keats's records in his 3 February 1818 letter to John Hamilton Reynolds, found in *Norton Anthology of English Literature*, 7th ed., M. H. Abrams et al. (New York: W. W. Norton, 2000), 890–91.

13. Sarton, *Endgame*, 177. Subsequent references are given parenthetically in the text.

14. Sarton, *Encore*, 331.

15. See Sarton, *Encore*, 95. Since these conclusions on the presidency of George Bush and the Gulf War are included at the end of the

discussion on *Coming into Eighty* (chapter 3), I will not rehearse them again here. Subsequent references to *Encore* are given parenthetically in the text.

16. Because of Sherman's excellent compilations, I may be speaking relatively early in identifying Sarton's last publication as *Encore*.

17. Sarton, *At Eighty-Two* (New York: W. W. Norton, 1996), 27.

18. Heilbrun, *Last Gift of Time,* 84.

19. Sarton, *At Eighty-Two*, 9. Subsequent references are given parenthetically in the text.

20. In fact this is the only major difference Sarton cites between the Holocaust and Bosnia: in the Holocaust we did not know what was going on in the concentration camps; in Bosnia we know but seem unwilling or unable to do anything about it.

21. Sarton, *At Eighty-Two,* 139. Sarton's mastectomy is recounted in her journal *Recovering.*

22. Sarton, *At Eighty-Two,* 146. This recognition of the wish to die and the obvious corollary that suicide may be an option, along with the triumphant choice to live and celebrate another day, is paralleled in the opening chapter of Heilbrun's *Last Gift of Time.*

23. I have been unable to obtain a copy of this play for review in this volume.

24. Sarton, *At Eighty-Two,* 345.

BIBLIOGRAPHY

Works by May Sarton

Journals and Memoirs

I Knew a Phoenix. New York: W. W. Norton, 1954; London: P. Owen, 1963.

Plant Dreaming Deep. New York: W. W. Norton, 1968.

Journal of a Solitude. New York: W. W. Norton, 1973; London: Women's Press, 1973.

A World of Light. New York: W. W. Norton, 1976; London: Women's Press, 1996.

The House by the Sea. New York: W. W. Norton, 1976; London: Prior, 1977.

Recovering: A Journal. New York: W. W. Norton, 1980; London: Women's Press, 1997.

At Seventy. New York: W. W. Norton, 1984; London: Norton, 1984.

Honey in the Hive: Judy Matlack 1898–1982. Boston: Warren Publishing, 1988.

After the Stroke. New York: W. W. Norton, 1988; London: Women's Press, 1997.

Endgame: A Journal of the Seventy-Ninth Year. New York: W. W. Norton, 1992; London: Women's Press, 1993.

Encore: A Journal of the Eightieth Year. New York: W. W. Norton, 1993; London: Women's Press, 1993.

At Eighty-Two. New York: W. W. Norton, 1996; London: Women's Press, 1996.

Poetry

Encounter in April. Boston: Houghton Mifflin, 1937.

BIBLIOGRAPHY

Inner Landscape. Boston: Houghton Mifflin, 1939; London: Cresset Press, 1939.

The Lion and the Rose. New York: Rinehart, 1948.

The Leaves of the Tree. Mt. Vernon, Iowa: The English Club of Cornell College, 1950.

The Land of Silence. New York: Rinehart, 1953.

In Time Like Air. New York: Rinehart, 1958.

Cloud, Stone, Sun, Vine. New York: W. W. Norton, 1961.

A Private Mythology. New York: W. W. Norton, 1966.

As Does New Hampshire. Peterborough, N.H.: R. R. Smith, 1967.

A Grain of Mustard Seed. New York: W. W. Norton, 1971.

A Durable Fire. New York: W. W. Norton, 1972.

Halfway to Silence. New York: W. W. Norton, 1980; London: Women's Press, 1993.

Letters from Maine. New York: W. W. Norton, 1984.

The Silence Now. New York: W. W. Norton, 1988; London: W. W. Norton, 1989.

Collected Poems (1930–1993). New York: W. W. Norton, 1993. A collection of the most important poems published by Sarton through 1993.

Coming into Eighty. New York: W. W. Norton, 1994; London: Women's Press, 1995.

Novels

The Single Hound. New York: W. W. Norton, 1938; London: Cresset Press, 1938.

The Bridge of Years. New York: W. W. Norton, 1946; London: Women's Press, 1974.

The Shadow of a Man. New York: W. W. Norton, 1950; London: Cresset Press, 1951.

Shower of Summer Days. New York: W. W. Norton, 1952; London: Hutchinson, 1954.

BIBLIOGRAPHY

Faithful Are the Wounds. New York: W. W. Norton, 1955; London: V. Gollancz, 1955.

The Birth of a Grandfather. New York: W. W. Norton, 1957; London: V. Gollancz, 1957.

The Fur Person. New York: W. W. Norton, 1957; London: F. Muller, 1957.

The Small Room. New York: W. W. Norton, 1961; London: Women's Press, 1996.

Joanna and Ulysses. New York: W. W. Norton, 1963.

Mrs. Stevens Hears the Mermaids Singing. New York: W. W. Norton, 1965; London: Peter Owen, 1965.

Miss Pickthorn and Mr. Hare. New York: W. W. Norton, 1966; London: Dent, 1968.

The Poet and the Donkey. New York: W. W. Norton, 1969.

Kinds of Love. New York: W. W. Norton, 1970; London: W. W. Norton, 1970.

As We Are Now. New York: W. W. Norton, 1973; London: V. Gollancz & Women's Press, 1973.

Crucial Conversations. New York: W. W. Norton, 1975; London: V. Gollancz, 1975.

A Reckoning. New York: W. W. Norton, 1978; London: Women's Press, 1978.

Anger. New York: W. W. Norton, 1982; South Yarmouth, Mass.: Curley, 1982.

The Magnificent Spinster. New York: W. W. Norton, 1985; London: Women's Press, 1985.

The Education of Harriet Hatfield. New York: W. W. Norton, 1989; London: Women's Press, 1989.

Children's Books

Punch's Secret. New York: Harper & Row, 1974.

A Walk in the Woods. New York: Harper & Row, 1976.

BIBLIOGRAPHY

Collected Essays

Writings on Writing. Orono, Maine: Puckerbush Press, 1980; London: Women's Press, 1995.

Letters

Dear Juliette: Letters of May Sarton to Juliette Huxley. Ed. Susan Sherman. New York: W. W. Norton, 1999.
May Sarton: Selected Letters, 1916–1954. Vol. 1. Ed. Susan Sherman. New York: W. W. Norton, 1997.

Selected Interviews

Conversations with May Sarton. Ed. Earl G. Ingersoll. Jackson: University Press of Mississippi, 1991.
Todd, Janet. "Interview with May Sarton." In *Women Writers Talking,* ed. Janet Todd. New York: Holmes and Meier Publishers, 1983.

Forewords

Foreword to *Shattered Applause: The Lives of Eva La Gallienne,* by Robert A. Schanke. Carbondale: Southern Illinois University Press, 1992.

Secondary Sources on Sarton's Life and Work

Books and Collections

Limmer, Ruth. *What the Woman Lived: Selected Letters of Louise Bogan, 1920–1970.* New York: Harcourt Brace Jovanovich, 1973.

Contains thirty-six letters from Bogan to Sarton, some of which are in response to Sarton's letters to Bogan (these are printed in Sarton's *Selected Letters*). Valuable for its insight into the complex and intricate relationship between these two poets.

Bowles, Gloria. *Louise Bogan's Aesthetics of Limitation.* Bloomington: Indiana University Press, 1987. A discussion of Bogan's poetic technique, which influenced Sarton.

Drake, William. *The First Wave: Women Poets in America, 1915–1945.* New York: MacMillan, 1987. The final chapter offers an analysis of Sarton's and Bogan's poetry, seeing the style and innovations in their poetry as offering some of the most promising directions in postwar feminist verse.

Evans, Elizabeth. *May Sarton Revisited.* Boston: Twayne Publishers, 1989. Complimentary to my study of Sarton although Evans specifically explores Sarton's relevance to women.

Faderman, Lillian. *Surpassing the Love of Men: Romantic Friendship and Love between Women from the Renaissance to the Present.* New York: William Morrow, 1981. Following in the footsteps of Jeannette H. Foster, this study centers on expressions of love among women and includes an analysis of Sarton's novels.

Foster, Jeannette H. *Sex Variant Women in Literature.* Tallahassee: The Naiad Press, 1985. One of the early studies of lesbianism in literature, spanning the history of Western literature from Sappho to Sarton and beyond. Originally published in 1956, this later edition contains essays extending and revising the original study.

Frank, Elizabeth. *Louise Bogan: A Portrait.* New York: Alfred A. Knopf, 1985. Delves into the life and art of Sarton's close friend Bogan and offers some insight into their complex personal and artistic relationship.

Glendinning, Victoria. *Elizabeth Bowen.* New York: Alfred A. Knopf, 1978. A systematic study of Irish novelist Elizabeth Bowen with reference to her relationships with Sarton and the Bloomsbury group.

BIBLIOGRAPHY

Kallet, Marilyn, ed. *A House of Gathering: Poets on May Sarton's Poetry.* Knoxville: University of Tennessee Press, 1993. The best book-length study of Sarton's poetry, offering appreciative and celebratory essays on her achievements.

Heilbrun, Carolyn. *The Last Gift of Time: Life beyond Sixty.* New York: Ballantine Books, 1997. Heilbrun's chapter "A Unique Person" offers a sympathetic yet candid look at Sarton in her later life and career. One of the best biographical reflections on Sarton.

Hunting, Constance, ed. *A Celebration for May Sarton.* Orono, Maine: Puckerbush Press, 1994. Hunting's second collection of essays. Offers systematic criticism of Sarton's life and works.

————. *May Sarton: Woman and Poet.* Orono, Maine: Puckerbush Press, 1982. The first systematic critical study of Sarton's work beyond the introductory level. Suggests ways of reading Sarton's poetry and her life.

Nicolson, Nigel, and Joanne Trautmann, eds. *The Letters of Virginia Woolf.* Vol. 6: 1936–1941. New York: Harcourt Brace, 1980. Contains Woolf's early letters and advice to Sarton as a young novelist and poet.

Ostriker, Alicia Suskin. *Stealing the Language: The Emergence of Women's Poetry in America.* Boston: Beacon Press, 1986. A study of the differences in language use between male and female poets of the later twentieth century. Celebrates the emergence of the strong feminist voice that Sarton pioneered.

Peters, Margot. *May Sarton: A Biography.* New York: Alfred A. Knopf, 1997. The only biography of Sarton. An in-depth study of Sarton's personality and love affairs. Tends to revel in the scandalous nature of Sarton's life.

Sarton, May. "Letters from H. D." In *H. D.: Woman and Poet,* ed. Michael King. Orono, Maine: National Poetry Foundation, 1986. Includes several letters written to Sarton by the poet H. D. during World War II that discuss poetry and survival during the war.

BIBLIOGRAPHY

Schanke, Robert A. *Shattered Applause: The Lives of Eva La Galli-enne.* Carbondale: Southern Illinois University Press, 1992. A study of the life of Sarton's theatrical mentor and longtime friend La Gallienne, with special focus on her secret lesbian relationships. Sarton was interviewed extensively for this volume and shares some of the less savory aspects of her relationship with La Gallienne. She also wrote the foreword to the volume, which constitutes her last word on this relationship and that time of her life in the theater.

Sibley, Agnes. *May Sarton.* New York: Twayne, 1972. An excellent study of Sarton's writing up through the late 1960s.

Swartzlander, Susan, and Marilyn R. Mumford, eds. *That Great San-ity: Critical Essays on May Sarton.* Ann Arbor: University of Michigan Press, 1993. An attempt to include Sarton's work within the critical conversation about the feminist movement. Particularly insightful are the essays by Mumford, Swartzlander, and Carol Virginia Pohli.

Uncollected Scholarly Articles

Anderson, Dawn Holt. "May Sarton's Women." In *Images of Women in Fiction: Feminist Perspectives,* ed. Susan Koppelman Cornillon. Bowling Green, Ohio: Bowling Green University Popular Press, 1972. An early feminist reading of Sarton's depiction of women in her fiction.

Bakerman, Jane S. "'Kinds of Love': Love and Friendship in the Nov-els of May Sarton." *Critique* 22, no. 2 (1978): 83–91. An overview of friendship and its move into passion in several of Sarton's mid-career novels.

Curry, Renée. "May Sarton and Elizabeth Bishop: Certain of a Revi-sionist Age." *Puckerbush Review* (winter 1993): 51–57. Studies Sarton's and Bishop's revisions of the metaphysical tradition.

BIBLIOGRAPHY

Eder, Doris L. "Woman Writer: May Sarton's *Mrs. Stevens Hears The Mermaids Singing*." *The International Journal of Women's Studies* 1, no. 2 (1978): 150–58. Explores the relationship between Sarton and her fictional character Hilary Stevens.

Gaskill, Gail. "The Mystery of the Mother and the Muse in May Sarton's *Mrs. Stevens Hears the Mermaids Singing*." *NMAL: Notes on Modern American Literature* 8 (spring–summer 1984): Item 7. Explores the female artist's uniqueness as depicted in Sarton's most important novel.

Hoffman, Nancy Yanes. "Sartonalia: Signposts and Destinations." *Southwest Review* (summer 1977): 258–67. A mid-1970s survey of Sarton's fiction, with predictions of where she might turn next.

Klein, Kathleen Gregory. "Aging and Dying in the Novels of May Sarton." *Critique* 24, no. 3 (1983): 150–57. Discusses when and how Sarton's characters age and die.

Malpezzi, Frances R. "'Clear Geometric Praise': Two Ekphrastic Poems of May Sarton." *Cithara* 35 (May 1996): 18–25. A study of Sarton's poems "Nativity" and "Annunciation" and their relationship to the visual arts.

Miner, Valerie. "Spinning Friends: May Sarton's Literary Spinsters." In *Old Maids to Radical Spinsters: Unmarried Women in the Twentieth-Century Novel,* ed. Laura L. Doan. Urbana: University of Illinois Press, 1991. Explores spinsters in Sarton's novels.

Otis, Danielle. "Sarton's 'Because What I Want Most is Permanence.'" *Explicator* 47 (1989): 55–57. A study of emotional balance in Sarton's poem.

Springer, Marlene. "As We Shall Be: May Sarton and Aging." *Frontiers* 5, no. 3 (1980): 46–49. Examines the needs of the elderly as seen through Sarton's fiction.

Stout, Janis P. "A Wordless Balm: Silent Communication in the Novels of May Sarton." *Essays in Literature* 20, no. 2 (1993): 310–23. Explicates Sarton's use of silences that speak in several of her novels.

BIBLIOGRAPHY

Straw, Deborah. "Tea with Virginia: Woolf as an Early Mentor to May Sarton." In *Virginia Woolf Miscellanies: Proceedings of the First Annual Conference on Virginia Woolf,* ed. Mark Hussey and Vara Neverow Turk, 45–47. New York: Pace University Press, 1992. The only systematic study—albeit short—of Woolf's influence on Sarton's fiction.

Wheelock, Martha. "May Sarton: A Metaphor for My Life, My Work, and My Art." In *Between Women: Biographers, Novelists, Critics, Teachers, and Artists Write about Their Work on Women,* ed. Carol Ascher, Louise DeSalvo, and Sara Ruddick. Boston: Beacon Press, 1984. A look at Sarton and her nonfiction through the eyes of her close friend Wheelock.

Woodward, Kathleen. "May Sarton and Fictions of Old Age." *Women and Literature* 1 (1980): 108–27. Explores the connections between feminism and aging in Sarton's novels.

Wyatt-Brown, Anne M. "Another Model of the Aging Writer: Sarton's Politics of Old Age." In *Aging and Gender in Literature: Studies in Creativity,* ed. Anne M. Wyatt-Brown and Janice Rosen. Charlottesville: University Press of Virginia, 1993. A reading of aging in Sarton's final novel, *The Education of Harriet Hatfield.*

INDEX

DATE DUE

NOV 0 5 2007			